# Cesar Chavez

THE IMPORTANCE OF

# Cesar Chavez

These and other titles are included in The Importance
Of biography series:

THE IMPORTANCE OF

# Cesar Chavez

by
Linda Jacobs Altman

Lucent Books, P.O. Box 289011, San Diego, CA 92198-9011

Library of Congress Cataloging-in-Publication Data

Altman, Linda Jacobs, 1943-
    Cesar Chavez / by Linda Jacobs Altman.
        p.  cm.—(The Importance of)
    Includes bibliographical references and index.
    Summary: The life and historical significance of the
Mexican American labor organizer who demanded rights for
migrant farm workers
        ISBN 1-56006-071-9  (Lib. ed. : alk. pap.)
        1. Chavez, Cesar, 1927–1993—Juvenile literature. 2. Trade-
unions—Migrant agricultural laborers—United States—
Officials and employees—Biography—Juvenile literature.
3. Labor leaders—United States—Biography—Juvenile
literature. 4. Mexican Americans—Biography—Juvenile literature. 5. United Farm Workers—History—Juvenile literature.
[1. Chavez, Cesar, 1927–1993. 2. Labor leaders. 3. Mexican
Americans—Biography.    4. United Farm Workers—History]
I. Title. II. Title: Importance of Cesar Chavez. III. Series.
HD6509.C48A68      1996
331.88'13'092—dc20
[B]                                                      95-11734
                                                            CIP
                                                             AC

Copyright 1996 by Lucent Books, Inc., P.O. Box 289011,
San Diego, California, 92198-9011

Printed in the U.S.A.

# Contents

# Foreword

THE IMPORTANCE OF biography series deals with individuals who have made a unique contribution to history. The editors of the series have deliberately chosen to cast a wide net and include people from all fields of endeavor. Individuals from politics, music, art, literature, philosophy, science, sports, and religion are all represented. In addition, the editors did not restrict the series to individuals whose accomplishments have helped change the course of history. Of necessity, this criterion would have eliminated many whose contribution was great, though limited. Charles Darwin, for example, was responsible for radically altering the scientific view of the natural history of the world. His achievements continue to impact the study of science today. Others, such as Chief Joseph of the Nez Percé, played a pivotal role in the history of their own people. While Joseph's influence does not extend much beyond the Nez Percé, his nonviolent resistance to white expansion and his continuing role in protecting his tribe and his homeland remain an inspiration to all.

These biographies are more than factual chronicles. Each volume attempts to emphasize an individual's contributions both in his or her own time and for posterity. For example, the voyages of Christopher Columbus opened the way to European colonization of the New World. Unquestionably, his encounter with the New World brought monumental changes to both Europe and the Americas in his day. Today, however, the broader impact of Columbus's voyages is being critically scrutinized. *Christopher Columbus,* as well as every biography in The Importance Of series, includes and evaluates the most recent scholarship available on each subject.

Each author includes a wide variety of primary and secondary source quotations to document and substantiate his or her work. All quotes are footnoted to show readers exactly how and where biographers derive their information, as well as provide stepping stones to further research. These quotations enliven the text by giving readers eyewitness views of the life and times of each individual covered in The Importance Of series.

Finally, each volume is enhanced by photographs, bibliographies, chronologies, and comprehensive indexes. For both the casual reader and the student engaged in research, The Importance Of biographies will be a fascinating adventure into the lives of people who have helped shape humanity's past and present, and who will continue to shape its future.

## Important Dates in the Life of Cesar Chavez

**1927**

Born March 31 near Yuma, Arizona.

**1944**

Enlists in the navy during World War II.

**1948**

Marries Helen Fabela.

**1952**

Is recruited by Fred Ross to work for the Community Service Organization.

**1958**

Becomes national director of CSO.

**1962**

Resigns from CSO to start a farm workers union.

**1965**

National Farm Workers Association (NFWA) enters grape strike on September 16.

**1966**

Campesinos' march begins March 17 in Delano, California, and arrives in Sacramento April 11; NFWA merges with the Agricultural Workers Organizing Committee (AWOC) to become the United Farm Workers Organizing Committee (UFWOC) of the AFL-CIO.

**1968**

Begins fast for nonviolence on February 15; breaks fast on March 10 by taking bread from Senator Robert Kennedy.

**1970**

UFWOC reaches contract agreements with most grape growers.

**1972**

Fasts for twenty-four days to protest repressive labor laws; UFWOC drops "Organizing Committee" from its name when it is chartered by AFL-CIO; Chavez elected president.

**1975**

Helps California governor Jerry Brown pass farm worker legislation.

**1984**

Announces international grape boycott.

**1988**

Fasts for thirty-six days to protest pesticide use.

**1990**

Signs agreement with Mexican government allowing Mexican farm workers in the United States to provide medical benefits to their families in Mexico.

**1993**

Dies in San Luis, Arizona, on April 23.

# The Road Less Traveled

Cesar Chavez was a small, soft-eyed man with a private life so ordinary some might call it boring. He never finished high school or became rich and powerful, yet he stood up to the combined powers of government and corporate agriculture to demand a better life for migrant farm workers. The organization he founded eventually became the United Farm Workers of America (UFW), the first successful union for workers who have been called "the most unorganizable, most powerless people on earth."[1]

## A Gentle Crusader

Though Chavez worked mostly in California, he mounted boycotts that spread throughout the nation. In his unquestioning dedication to the cause of migrant workers, he possessed a power that journalist Sam Stanton described as "a combination of quiet charisma and stubbornness [that swayed] people to his cause, whether they were workers he persuaded to join the union or high-powered attorneys he talked into going to work for him at the wage of $10.00 a week."[2]

The traits that helped Chavez to succeed also had a negative side, however.

The charisma that made him so effective threatened to turn UFW into a personality cult that existed in the shadow of its founder; the stubbornness that challenged every obstacle could slip over the line into inflexibility.

Long after the union had grown too big for one man to manage, Chavez refused to delegate authority to others. "If a car in Salinas needed a new tire," said

*Cesar Chavez's unwavering dedication to helping migrant farm workers made him a working-class hero to thousands of people around the world.*

former union worker Aristeo Zambrano, "we had to check with Cesar in La Paz. He controlled every detail of union business."[3]

## "A Very Great Man"

Even those who had trouble working with Chavez admired his dedication and recognized his honesty. When he died on April 23, 1993, flags in California's state capitol building flew at half staff. Supporters and opponents alike honored the memory of this unassuming field-worker who challenged the multimillion dollar agricultural industry.

"Society has lost a very great man," said Dolores Huerta, former vice president of UFW, and a founding member. "Cesar proved to the world that poor people can solve their problems if they stick together, and he showed the rest of society how they can participate and help the downtrodden."[4]

In his long and selfless career, Cesar Chavez was different things to different people. To activists he was a social reformer, moved by the injustices around him. To labor leaders he was a union organizer, trying to bring the benefits of collective bargaining to agricultural workers. To religious people, he was a spiritual crusader trying to do God's work. Chavez appealed to the conscience of a nation through strikes, peace marches, and boycotts. His methods were masterful, and always nonviolent.

In the early seventies, UFW had a hundred thousand members working under collective bargaining agreements. By the early nineties, there were only twenty thousand, and much of the union's political and economic power was gone. Still, the struggle had not been in vain. A number of public and private agencies concerned themselves with farm worker issues, consumers were more aware of the people whose labor put food on their tables, and Chavez himself had become a living legend who was often compared to M. K. Gandhi and Martin Luther King Jr.

When Chavez died in April 1993, a nation mourned that legend; a widow and eight grown children mourned the man. President Bill Clinton eulogized this gentle, soft-spoken leader as "an authentic hero to millions of people throughout the world."[5]

What molded and motivated Cesar Chavez? How did he rise from humble field-worker to legendary hero? The answers to those questions reveal neither saint nor superman. Chavez was a human being who knew what it meant to live with poverty and prejudice; he saw a need and set out to fill it to the best of his ability. The story of that commitment to the poorest of the poor is also the life story of this remarkable man.

# 1 Hard Times

Cesar Estrada Chavez was born March 31, 1927, near Yuma, Arizona. His parents, Librado and Juana Chavez, owned a small grocery store with attached living quarters, a separate mechanic's garage, and even a pool hall with a little counter that sold sodas, cigarettes, and candy. Half the people in the area around Yuma were related to the Chavez family in one way or another and gladly did their shopping at Librado's little store. Business was good in those days, and life was relatively secure.

Then came the stock market crash of 1929. In only a few hours of trading, stock that had been worth thousands of dollars became worthless, and the American

*When Librado Chavez lost his business in the midst of the Great Depression, the Chavezes were forced to move back to the family farm (pictured) near Yuma, Arizona.*

## The Family Farm

*The farm that Librado Chavez lost during the Great Depression had been home to the Chavez family since long before Cesar was born. In* Sal Si Puedes: Cesar Chavez and the New American Revolution, *author Peter Matthiessen describes the much-loved farm.*

"As a homesteader [Cesar's grandfather] acquired some 160 acres of sage and mesquite desert in the North Gila River Valley about twenty miles northeast of Yuma, part of which he built carefully into a farm. . . . According to Cesar, his grandfather admired the big Mexican haciendas, and since he had nine sons and six daughters to help out, he designed his house accordingly. It lasted a half century and might have lasted indefinitely in that dry climate had the roof been of tile instead of adobe, because the walls were twenty-four inches thick. The farm was cool in summer, warm in winter, with wide barn areas for livestock food and farm equipment; it stood on a slope against the hills, with a laundry-and-wood shed on one side and a garden on the other."

economy plunged into the Great Depression. Banks failed; businesses went bankrupt; millions of hard-working people lost their jobs.

The Chavez grocery store felt the pinch right away. All of a sudden, the relatives who had been such good customers did not have enough money to feed their families. Librado Chavez was not a man who could stand by and watch children starve; he sold groceries on credit for as long as he could. By 1932, however, he could no longer make payments on his property. He had to sell the store at a big loss and move back to the Chavez family farm, outside Yuma.

For Cesar and the other children, this move was not a tragedy; they had visited the old adobe farmhouse many times, so it felt like home to them. At first, life on the farm was comfortable—Librado worked the land, while Juana raised chickens. Cesar recalled selling the eggs for five or six cents a dozen. He told Jacques Levy:

But then the depression got worse and we couldn't sell anything. People didn't even have five cents. Because there was simply no money around, everything was bartered. Mom would send us with a basket of eggs to someone, and we would return with bread or flour or something else in exchange. . . . [O]n the farm during the depression we didn't suffer the way people in the city or migrants suffered. We had vegetables, eggs, milk, and chicken, and we had as much as we wanted.[6]

Cesar had no idea how shaky the family's financial situation had become. To him, life was still warm and safe, marked by his mother's simple but profound wisdom and unquestioning religious faith. Like most Mexican-American parents, Juana Chavez was a great believer in using *dichos* (sayings, or proverbs) and *consejos* (advice) in the moral training of her children.

Though Cesar was too young to understand his mother's meaning in those days, he sensed that it was deep and wise and worthy of respect. Her sayings were about obedience and honesty and solving problems in nonviolent ways: It takes two to fight, one can't do it alone was one of her favorites.

"When I look back, I see her sermons had tremendous impact on me," Cesar recalled. "I didn't know it was nonviolence then, but after reading Gandhi, St. Francis, and other exponents of nonviolence, I began to clarify that in my mind."[7]

## An Outcast at School

Cesar learned more from listening to his mother and working on the farm than he learned at school. From his first days in class, he felt uncomfortable and strange. At home, he spoke Spanish and went barefoot all summer long. At school, speaking Spanish was against the rules and going without shoes was unthinkable, even when the weather was hot. Cesar understood well enough about the shoes, but he did not understand why it was wrong to speak Spanish.

Many a time, he forgot about the no-Spanish rule, or just became frustrated with English and spoke in the language of his home and family. Getting caught brought instant punishment: a ruler across the knuckles, a stiff wooden paddle on the rear end. Cesar soon realized that speaking Spanish and being Mexican made him an outcast among his Anglo schoolmates. It was a painful lesson that shook his confidence and made him dread going to school.

Even with his problems in the classroom, Cesar was happy enough with his life on the farm. There was something changeless and comfortable about the place. The idea of leaving it never entered his mind, not even when he saw his father worrying more and more about paying taxes on the house and the land. In 1939 the county government said that Librado Chavez owed nearly $4,000 in property taxes. When he couldn't pay, the Board of Supervisors took over the farm and sold it at auction. Years later, Chavez recalled the heartbreak and horror that followed:

> [A] big red tractor came to the farm . . . it tore up the soil, leveling it, and destroyed the trees, pushing them over like they were nothing . . . each tree, of course, means quite a bit to you when you're young. . . . We grew up there, saw them every day, and they were alive, they were friends. When we saw the bulldozer just uprooting those trees, it was tearing at us too.[8]

The trees were not the only things to be uprooted that February; the Chavez family packed their scant belongings and took to the road, heading for the "promised land" known as California. Memories were all Cesar had left of the town where he was born and the farm that had been in his family for years.

Not all those memories were happy; Cesar never lost sight of how it felt to be called "a dumb Mexican," or to get his

*A child working to help his family hauls onions from the field. Migrant farm workers lead difficult lives, often not knowing when or where they will find their next job.*

knuckles rapped for speaking Spanish, or to watch while a tractor destroyed his home. These memories went with him as the Chavez family headed for an unknown future.

## The Migrant Life

The Chavezes arrived in California with $40 and no prospects for work or housing in sight. They joined thousands of other families who had lost everything in the depression, and now traveled up and down the state of California, looking for work in the fields. When they did find a job, the whole family had to work; wages were so low that Librado and Juana could not make enough money for rent and gro-

ceries without help from the children.

Even with everybody working, life was an unending struggle. Back in Yuma, none of the family had gone hungry or slept on a cold floor. There were always vegetables from Librado's garden, eggs from Juana's chickens, and the rambling adobe house that was cool in summer and warm in winter. Cesar missed all of that. In California, he was hungry most of the time and so was everybody else in the family.

As migrant workers, the Chavezes often had to live in grim labor camps where there was only one restroom for the whole camp and no water, plumbing, or electricity in the cabins. They considered themselves lucky if they could live in the nearest *barrio* (low-income, Spanish-speaking neighborhood) rather than stay in the camp. The barrios were known for sub-

## The Legacy of Juana Chavez

*Only in later life did Cesar realize the profound effect his mother had on his thinking, especially regarding non-violence and quiet courage. In* Cesar Chavez: Autobiography of La Causa, *Chavez describes his mother to Jacques Levy.*

"My mom kept the family together. She was the sort of woman who had time for her children, who would talk with us. She used many dichos—proverbs—and they all had a real purpose. 'What you do to others, others do to you' was one of them. 'He who holds the cow, sins as much as he who kills her.' 'If you're in the honey, some of it will stick to you.' Though she was illiterate, she had a tremendous memory. I think most illiterate persons do because they must rely upon their memories. . . . When I look back, I see her sermons had tremendous impact on me. I didn't know it was nonviolence then, but after reading Gandhi, St. Francis, and other exponents of non-violence, I began to clarify that in my mind."

standard housing, dirt streets, and lack of sewer services, but at least the houses were roomier and more cheerful than shacks in a labor camp. Many barrio houses didn't have indoor bathrooms, but there was usually a real kitchen where Juana could fix meals, and a yard where the children could play.

Between jobs, the family couldn't afford any rent at all, so they lived out of the broken-down car that Librado kept together with junkyard parts and a dash of imagination. Without that car they could not have moved from one job to the next. Even with a serviceable car and Librado's quiet determination to survive, however, the search for work was filled with problems. Often the only way to get a job was to work through contractors or recruiters. Some of these "middlemen" were actually crew bosses. They could make a deal to harvest a grower's crop, then hire their own pickers and supervise the work. Others got paid just for recruiting workers and sending them to the personnel manager of a particular farm.

A few of the contractors were decent, hard-working people who did a service for growers and workers alike. Most of them were greedy and dishonest, promising more than they could ever hope to deliver and caring nothing for the human misery they caused. The workers called them *coyotes*, after the cowardly scavengers of the deserts, who survive on the work of other animals.

Librado Chavez was an easy target for *coyotes*. Because he was honest with others, he expected others to be honest with him; he believed what the *coyotes* said and acted upon it, often with near-disastrous results. Cesar never forgot the time his father got a firsthand lesson in the tactics of *coyotes*. The family had stopped to buy gas outside the town of Salinas, when a man told them about a job picking peas, just a short drive up the coast to Half Moon Bay. It offered good wages and decent housing for anyone who was willing to work. The man gave Librado an official-looking card and told him to present it to the foreman when the family reported for work.

The Chavezes went straight to the farm, only to find out that wages were half what the recruiter had promised. Worse yet, there were too many workers with that little card, and no housing for anyone. It turned out that the contractor earned $20 for every family he recruited, so he thought nothing of sending a hundred workers to fill a dozen jobs. From his

*Upon finishing the eighth grade, Chavez (pictured here on his graduation day) quit school for good.*

point of view, it was good business. By the same token, the grower was glad to pay the recruiter multiple fees because having more people than jobs meant that wages could be kept down. If anyone balked at the low pay, there were ten more workers waiting to take his place.

Librado wanted better for his family. He joined an agricultural workers union, hoping that group action could bring higher wages, decent housing, and a safer workplace. That union failed, but Librado never gave up hope that someday, somewhere, another would succeed.

In late autumn of the family's first year on the road, they got jobs in the walnut groves near the southern California town of Oxnard. It was the last harvest of the season; when it ended there would be no fieldwork for anyone until the following spring. Librado and Juana decided to stay put for the winter. They didn't have enough money to rent a place to stay, so they set up a tent near La Colonia, a poor, unincorporated settlement just outside the city limits.

Being from the dry climate of Arizona, the family had never experienced anything like the wet, cold, foggy conditions of a winter on the shores of the Pacific Ocean. In the constant dampness of Oxnard, nothing ever dried and nobody slept warm. By the time Librado and Juana realized how difficult that winter would be, it was too late to leave. In any event, they couldn't afford gas for the car, so they settled in and tried to make the best of a bad situation. One of the first things they did was enroll the children in school.

Cesar was miserable at the thought of going to a strange new school. In Yuma, he had been punished for speaking Spanish, but at least he belonged somewhere; he was the boy from the Chavez farm. In

## The Way of Nonviolence

*In her book* The Peaceable Revolution, *author Betty Schechter explained the principles of nonviolence that shaped the life and work of Cesar Chavez.*

"Peaceable Revolution. The words seem to contradict each other. Historically, revolutions have been violent, bloody uprisings of people who . . . united and by the force of arms attempted to change the order of things . . . In the twentieth century, however, another kind of revolution has been fought. Attacks have been launched and battles won by men and women whose most powerful weapon was the conscience of their opponents. Militant in their determination to win, they have, nonetheless, refused to resort to violence . . . they have sought not conquest but reconciliation. Theirs have been peaceable revolts based on the idea and the method of nonviolent resistance to evil. . . . In the history of man's unending quest for justice they point the way to a new method of protest, an effective method and a bloodless one."

Oxnard, he was only a migrant, who lived in a tent and did not even have a regular address. Cesar and his brother Richard were fair game for schoolyard bullies who taunted them for their shabby clothes, for being poor, for living in a tent.

As a migrant, Cesar never stayed anywhere long enough to make friends; he once counted sixty-five different elementary schools that he had attended at one time or another. Upon finishing eighth grade, he quit school for good.

Two years later he joined the navy. The year was 1944, and World War II was still being waged in Europe and in the Pacific. Cesar was seventeen years old, with no real prospects, and the navy offered an escape from the drudgery of the fields. When he returned home at the end of the war, the only job he could find was picking grapes in the vineyards of Delano, California. It was there he met Helen Fabela, who was to become his wife. After their marriage in 1948, Cesar wanted more than ever to find a job that was good and steady, a job with a future.

Again and again he tried, but nobody wanted to hire a twenty-one-year-old navy veteran with an eighth-grade education. He was forced back into the fields. Cesar looked around at the squalid migrant camps, the *coyotes* who cheated farm workers, and the growers who exploited them. The Great Depression had been over for a long time. America had fought and won a war, yet life for migrants had not changed. Librado Chavez had been right—something ought to be done. But what? In 1952 Cesar Chavez took his first steps toward answering that question.

# 2 The Way of a Man

Cesar and Helen Chavez eventually found their way to northern California, where they settled in the notorious San Jose barrio known as Sal Si Puedes, which roughly translated to "get out if you can."

Cesar lived across the street from his younger brother Richard. The men worked together in the apricot orchards and spent many an evening sitting on the porch, talking about the problems of the poor. Both remembered the hard and rootless life of their childhood: the dishonest contractors, the insensitive growers, the failed unions their father kept joining. Although he rarely discussed those matters with anyone outside the family, one day Chavez confided in the parish priest, Father McDonnell.

## Unexpected Opportunities

Father McDonnell was a scholar who spoke seven languages, yet he knew how to relate to ordinary people. He cared about farm workers, understood their problems, and possessed an extensive knowledge of labor history. Night after night, the priest and the idealistic young farm worker discussed doctrines of social justice: "I began going to the [Mexican laborers'] camps with him to help with Mass; to the city jail with him to talk to the prisoners—anything to be with him so he could tell me more about the farm labor movement,"[9] Chavez told writer Stan Steiner.

From these talks, Father McDonnell sensed the leadership abilities hidden within the intense young man who had become his unofficial apprentice. When the Community Service Organization (CSO) wanted someone to build a chapter in Sal Si Puedes, the priest didn't have to think twice before recommending Chavez for the job.

CSO was the brainchild of Saul Alinsky, a recognized master of nonviolent confrontational politics. It was represented on the West Coast by a tall, intense young man named Fred Ross. Unfortunately, Ross's efforts to organize a chapter in Sal Si Puedes came on the heels of several university studies of the same barrio. Every institution of higher learning in the Bay Area had sent well-dressed Anglo graduate students to study the people and their way of life.

Years later, Chavez told writer Peter Matthiessen:

The [university] people used to talk about forty- or fifty-year patterns, and how did we eat our beans and tortillas, and whether we'd like to live in a two-bedroom house instead of a slum room, things like that. They try to make us real different, you know, because it spices up their studies when they do that. I thought this guy [Ross] meant to snoop like all the rest. We didn't have anything else in our experience to go by; we were being pushed around by all these studies.[10]

## Chavez and the Neighborhood Organizer

One afternoon in 1952, Fred Ross showed up unannounced at the Chavezes' front door, talking about making things better in the barrio and asking to meet with Cesar. When Helen said he was not at home, the stranger smiled politely, wished her a good evening, and promised to return.

"In those days," Chavez told Peter Matthiessen, "when a gringo wanted to see you, it was something special; we never heard anything from whites unless it was the police."[11] Helen Chavez didn't think this particular gringo was a policeman, so Cesar figured he must be another researcher, coming around to ask more dumb questions.

He began to play a kind of game; Fred Ross had said he would be back the next evening, so Cesar hid across the street at Richard's house, and watched the gringo come to the door, talk a moment with Helen, and then leave. Cesar thought that would be the end of it, but Ross didn't give up. He came back again and again, and each time Cesar arranged to be out of the house. Finally, Helen got tired of making excuses. If her husband wanted to be

*Fred Ross, a representative of the CSO, came to the barrio where Chavez lived to organize the residents so they could fight the poverty and hardships that plagued their neighborhood.*

rid of this persistent caller, he would have to take care of it himself.

Seeing little choice in the matter, Chavez agreed to meet with Fred Ross. He expected another sociologist, or perhaps another do-gooder who thought he could solve the problems of the barrio with canned food and secondhand clothes. But Fred Ross was not like that at all; he seemed entirely sincere about wanting to help the people of the barrio to help themselves. He had the good sense not to come to Sal Si Puedes dressed in a suit and driving a late-model car. His clothes were clean but rumpled, and his car had seen better days. Most impressive of all, he spoke fluent Spanish—not the classroom Castilian that most Anglos learned, but the down-to-earth, colloquial language of the barrio.

Chavez was impressed in spite of himself, but still he was more interested in getting rid of his visitor than in listening to what the other man had to say. When Ross asked him to invite some friends for an organizational meeting, Chavez knew just what to do. He rounded up some of the roughest men in the barrio, bought plenty of beer, and arranged a signal: they could start "getting nasty" when Chavez switched his cigarette from left hand to right.

## The First Meeting

Everyone was looking forward to a good time when Fred Ross arrived to begin the meeting. To Chavez's surprise, however, Ross made a lot of sense. He did not spout high-sounding theories or talk down to "the poor Mexicans." He spoke clearly, simply, and with the power of absolute conviction.

"He knew the problems as well as we did," Chavez told Peter Matthiessen. "He wasn't confused about the problems like so many people who want to help the poor." Some of the men became nervous, waiting for the fun to start, but Chavez never got around to moving his cigarette that night. Fred Ross was for real: "[Ross]

did such a good job of explaining how poor people could build power that I could even taste it, I could *feel* it . . . [it was] like digging a hole; there's nothing complicated about it!"[12]

When Fred left to conduct another organizational meeting, Chavez made hasty apologies to his other guests and went along. The experience was an unforgettable call to action. At last, Chavez had found a way to do more than complain about poverty and hardship. He was doing something important, something to help the farm workers who crowded the barrios and poverty-pockets all over California.

The work was not easy. Every time things seemed to go smoothly, a problem popped up to challenge Chavez's growing skills. When he was chairman of the voter registration project in San Jose, the first order of business was to find volunteers to serve as deputy registrars. The job was unexpectedly difficult, though. Of the sixteen friends he first recruited, not one could qualify as a deputy registrar. Some did not read well enough, in English or in Spanish. Others were ineligible because they had been convicted of felonies.

Chavez refused to give up. Perhaps his friends could not be registrars, but they could still be involved. They could knock on doors, they could persuade others to register, and they could help get out the vote come election day. Chavez and his hard-working friends covered the barrio, contacting almost every household in Sal Si Puedes. The project was an outstanding success, and so was the leadership of Cesar Chavez. His natural abilities began to shine through the quiet, unassuming manner. Before long, he was hired as a CSO staff member at a salary of $35 per week.

*Community Service Organization volunteers persuade barrio residents to register to vote. The volunteers' goal was to make sure the voices in the barrio were heard through their vote.*

## A Learning Experience

For the first eight months in his new position, Chavez worked in familiar territory around San Jose, dealing with people he knew in situations he understood. He continued using informal "house meetings," where nobody worried about parliamentary procedure and the group was small enough for everyone to have a say. Fred Ross had originated this technique; Cesar Chavez helped to develop it into a powerful tool for social change.

He became so adept at community organizing that CSO sent him to start a new chapter in Oakland. Though Oakland is not far from San Jose, Chavez had never

lived there; he did not know the community, or have the slightest idea what it needed. At the beginning, every house meeting was an overwhelming experience. Chavez was small, slight, and looked a good deal younger than his twenty-five years. He was certain that these characteristics would be liabilities for a community organizer.

His self-doubt was so painful that he would drive back and forth in front of the house where a meeting was to be held, worrying about what to say. Finally, he would park the car and slip inside, huddling in a corner until he had to step forward and take charge of the proceedings. It took courage for him to continue working in those early days, but he learned

*During the 1950s, Senator Joseph McCarthy launched an attack on activities he considered un-American. Chavez, whose bold actions were not typical of most Mexican Americans at that time, might easily have been seen as a troublemaker in such turbulent times, but he was undaunted by the anticommunist views spreading across the nation.*

from every meeting and gained confidence along the way. Over the next few years, he established CSO chapters in Madera, Bakersfield, and other farm towns in California and Arizona.

## A Climate of Suspicion

It was not the safest time to be doing such work. In the early 1950s, the cold war with the Soviet Union was in full swing, and the world was still dazed by the horrors of Auschwitz and Hiroshima. The antidote to fascism on the one hand and communism on the other was an uncompromising red-white-and-blue Americanism. Writer Todd Gitlin comments on this period:

> The affluent society was awash with fears of the uncontrollable. . . . The daily newspaper, the TV news, *Time* and *Life* and *Reader's Digest,* and at school the *Weekly Reader,* were all full

of thick red arrows and black tides swooping and oozing across the West. The supporters of Senator Joseph McCarthy feared the Communist Party of the United States of America. Liberal and left-wing enclaves feared McCarthyism. Conservatives feared social dissolution, immorality, rock 'n' roll, even fluoridation.[13]

As head of the House Committee on Un-American Activities, Senator Joseph McCarthy chaired an investigation that soon became a witch-hunt, violating, for many, the rights it was supposed to protect. For the first time in history, television was on hand to bring the proceedings into living rooms all over the country. The hearings became a national spectacle, leading self-appointed guardians of democracy to look askance at anyone who dared to speak out for unpopular causes.

A Mexican American who went around the barrios telling poor people to vote was at best a troublemaker, at worst a "tool of the international Communist conspiracy." Chavez knew about this climate of suspicion, but he never let it stop him from doing what he had promised to do. He continued his work registering voters and organizing citizenship classes, bringing hope and self-determination to the grim, dusty streets of California's barrios.

Because he refused to be cowed by the anticommunist views that spread across the nation, Chavez sometimes ran afoul of his own organization. Walk softly, friends told him; do not ask too much or complain too loudly. When he ignored these warnings, the Madera chapter of CSO began a secret investigation of his public and private life for any hint of communist sympathies. They wanted to show the Anglo world that they, too, were patriotic Americans. In due course, Chavez learned of the investigation and simply told the embarrassed CSO staffers to bring their charges into the open, rather than sneak around behind his back. The matter ended, then and there.

## The Power of Peace

Other problems weren't so easily overcome. Despite a natural flair for leadership, Chavez lacked the academic background to feel comfortable in the role of social reformer. Therefore he began reading everything he could find that looked as if it might be useful.

He studied labor history to learn about organization, negotiation, and collective bargaining, and then turned to the tactics of such nonviolent reformers as Henry David Thoreau. In 1846 when slavery was still a fact of American life and the government was entangled in a questionable war against Mexico, Thoreau refused to pay his taxes, in protest. He went to jail over a $1.50 assessment he could easily have afforded to pay. To him, it was a matter of principle:

> [W]hen a sixth of the population of a nation which has undertaken to be the refuge of liberty are slaves, and a whole country is unjustly overrun and conquered by a foreign army, and subjected to military law, I think that it is not too soon for honest men to rebel and revolutionize. What makes this duty the more urgent is the fact that the country so overrun is not our own, but ours is the invading army.[14]

Thoreau explored the concept of peaceful rebellion in his famous essay "Civil Disobedience." Years after his death, that slim book inspired reformers who wanted to change society with ideas rather than bullets. In India, M. K. Gandhi used those principles in the long struggle for independence from the British empire. In the United States, Martin Luther King Jr. used them to help bring an end to the racial segregation that denied African Americans their constitutional rights.

As Chavez read about what Dr. King called "noncooperation with evil," his vague desire to help farm workers shifted and changed and took a more definite shape. He began to see that those unions his father had joined hadn't worked because they tried to organize the fields the same way industrial unions organized the factories.

Workers with steady jobs and permanent homes could build a union complete with officers, negotiating teams, strike committees, perhaps even local hiring halls. Migrant farm workers never stayed anywhere long enough to build such a base. What they needed was a union that depended on a powerful idea rather than a permanent location. A commitment to nonviolent change was something the people could take with them, the way they took their love of family and their stubborn determination to endure the hardships of migrant life.

## Foundations for Action

Traditional Mexican culture regards endurance as a virtue, akin in many ways to the honored religious traditions of sainthood and martyrdom. The verb *aguantar* means to bear, to endure, to put up with; the noun form, *aguante*, is fortitude, patience, endurance. As author Earl Shorris observes:

> Living according to the concepts of *aguantar* . . . one can get along perfectly well in a small, very stable society, in a village culture. To compete, to be acquisitive, to be selfish, the traits valued in a modern capitalist society, have no place in a village culture. It is a gentler but more formal place, one in which the rules of society, which accommodate themselves to the laws of nature, are observed more carefully than in a tumultuous modern setting.[15]

In the barrios and migrant camps of the United States, *aguantar* brought fatalism and passivity to the older generation, and anger to the younger people who tried—and often failed—to live with one foot in each of two very different worlds:

---

### The Ways of Courage and Peace

*In* Stride Toward Freedom, *Martin Luther King Jr. explained his commitment to nonviolence with the eloquence that inspired Cesar Chavez.*

"In 1954 I ended my formal training with . . . divergent intellectual forces converging into a positive social philosophy. One of the main tenets of this philosophy was the conviction that nonviolent resistance was one of the most potent weapons available to oppressed people in their quest for social justice. At this time, however, I had merely an intellectual understanding and appreciation of the position, with no firm determination to organize it in a socially effective situation. . . . As the days unfolded, I came to see the power of nonviolence more and more. Living through the actual experience of the protest, nonviolence became . . . a commitment to a way of life."

---

"One of the social outgrowths of this situation," wrote historian Wayne Moquin, "was the formation of youth gangs in the *barrios*. The name they most commonly used to describe themselves was *Pachuco*, borrowed probably from the town of the same name in Mexico."[16]

Proud, angry, and poor, the Pachucos gained nationwide attention during the Zoot Suit Riots of 1943. In their baggy suits, shiny shoes, and wide-brim hats, they cut a swath through the barrio. The outlandish zoot suits did not last for long. Like most fads, this one burst upon the scene, then disappeared as suddenly as it had come. The anger it symbolized did not disappear.

The special genius of Cesar Chavez was to transform anger into positive action, and *aguantar* into strength for the struggle ahead. Through the mid-1950s, he studied what others had done and developed his own ideas. Finally, an assignment from CSO put those ideas to an unexpected test.

*After exploring the ideas of reformers such as Henry David Thoreau, M. K. Gandhi, and Martin Luther King Jr., Chavez wholly dedicated himself to bringing about change through nonviolent means.*

# 3 An Impossible Dream

When CSO decided to organize a chapter in Oxnard, the group assigned Chavez to the project. He returned to Oxnard in August 1958. It had been nearly twenty years since that first awful winter of his migrant life in a muddy field outside the town. This time, he wasn't a frightened child; he was a grown man with a family of his own and an important job to do.

He expected that job to revolve around the usual voter registration drives, neighborhood improvement projects, and citizenship classes, but the people of the barrio had something else in mind: Public Law 78, a federal statute that permitted growers to hire Mexican nationals to harvest American fields. The growers were eager to hire *braceros*, as the guest workers were called, because the Mexican laborers were not eligible to claim the minimum wage, nor were they covered by Social Security, workers' compensation, or other programs designed to benefit U.S. workers. People in the barrio, U.S. citizens and legal residents alike, hated Public Law 78 because it had the result of denying them employment in the only type of work many of them knew how to do.

*Mexican braceros ride a bus to America where they will work the fields. Growers were eager to employ braceros because they could pay them less than minimum wage and deny them benefits.*

## Public Law 78

*In his article* "The Grapes of Wrath— Vintage 1961," *which first appeared in* The Reporter *in 1961 and may also be found in* A Documentary History of the Mexican Americans, *edited by Wayne Moquin and Charles Van Doren, Arnold Mayer gives a clear overview of the impact of bracero programs on American agriculture.*

"Under P.L. 78, a total of 437,600 Mexican farm workers, known as braceros, were imported for seasonal work in 1959, mostly by growers of cotton, vegetables, fruits, and sugar beets. These growers represent less than two percent of America's farmers and are chiefly concentrated in California, Texas, Arizona, New Mexico, and Arkansas. But their farms, mainly large-scale operations, provided a disproportionate source of agricultural employment in the United States.

The huge influx of braceros has made it possible for these growers to keep wages down. (American farm workers earned an average of only $829 and got an average of only 138 days of work in 1959.) If domestic farm workers refuse the wage rate offered, the grower need not raise it. He tells the Federal government that he is unable to get workers (true, at his wage scale) and he then gets a group of braceros."

## The Bracero Debate

The bracero program had begun as an emergency measure during World War II, when growers faced labor shortages as a result of the war effort. Thus in 1942, the United States and Mexico completed the first of several agreements that brought Mexican farm workers to American fields. When the war ended, the growers did not want to lose this dependable source of cheap labor. To protect their advantage, the growers supported a series of agreements that culminated in 1951 with the passage of Public Law 78. On paper, the statute tied the bracero program to another crisis: this time, U.S. involvement in the Korean War. In practice, Public Law 78 established an ongoing program that did not end until 1965. Under its provisions, growers could request certification to hire braceros to compensate for a "manpower emergency" after they had made "reasonable efforts" to recruit domestic workers.

In its first year of operation, Public Law 78 brought 204,000 Mexican citizens to work in the United States; by the time Chavez arrived in Oxnard as a representative of CSO, braceros had almost entirely replaced domestic workers. For example, one Ventura County lemon harvest employed 2,500 braceros but only 150 domestics, and tomato fields near San Jose were worked by 8,530 braceros and 860 domestics.

*Braceros perform backbreaking work on a California farm. Chavez staged marches and rallies to protest Public Law 78, the often abused law that enabled growers to hire Mexican farmhands over domestic workers.*

In desperation, unemployed farm workers in Oxnard's Colonia district turned to CSO. To help them, Chavez first needed to define the problem. Under Public Law 78, the government was supposed to grant permission to hire braceros only if there were shortages of domestic labor. The growers of Oxnard seemed to have such shortages every harvest season; Chavez meant to find out why.

## Gathering Evidence

In the beginning of his fact-finding project, Chavez worked alone. For two weeks he arose before dawn and made his way to the labor camp, through the fog-shrouded chill of morning in Oxnard. When he asked for a job, the response was always the same: he needed a work card from the Farm Placement Office in Ventura, eight miles away.

By the time Chavez had obtained the work card and returned to Oxnard, that day's jobs had been filled and the crews were in the fields. If he came back the

next morning with the same card, the dispatcher called it outdated and sent him away. Chavez kept a record of names, dates, and times. At the end of two weeks, he had found out what he needed to know. He might not have enough evidence to prove his case to the government, but he had more than enough to get the people involved.

Using the CSO office as headquarters, Chavez gathered groups of unemployed farm workers willing to go through the complicated process of applying for work. Each morning, up to a dozen people carpooled to Ventura, where placement workers gave them official-looking forms to fill out. Chavez kept copies of every paper and a precise log of every encounter. When the file was thick with evidence, he was ready to move.

## Demonstrations and Protests

The first order of business was to dramatize the workers' plight in a way that would attract immediate public attention. Like

Thoreau withholding his taxes in New England to protest a war, or Martin Luther King Jr. boycotting buses in Montgomery, Alabama, to protest segregation, Cesar Chavez staged marches, rallies, and sit-ins in southern California to protest Public Law 78. He had a natural talent for the work, encouraging the timid, calming the violent, and making masterful use of symbolic acts and images to get his point across.

Through the harvest season of 1958 he led groups of workers to the fields, where in a silent appeal to conscience and fair play, they stationed themselves opposite the braceros who were doing jobs the U.S. workers had been denied. Chavez wasn't without sympathy for the braceros —they were poor and desperate and struggling to survive. No matter how much he suffered because of the Mexican workers,

he could not find it in his heart to resent them as individual human beings. His quarrel was with the system that victimized farm workers from both sides of the border. By playing the two groups against each other, growers kept both in line. Nobody dared to complain about working conditions or pay: Mexican Americans kept quiet because they might be replaced by Mexican nationals, and the braceros kept quiet because they could be sent home at the slightest hint of trouble. Only the growers benefited.

When the sit-ins had attracted enough attention, Chavez staged a protest march, complete with songs, slogans, and hand-lettered signs in Spanish and in English. The procession moved through the barrio and past the farms to the CSO office, for a grand finale. On a prearranged signal, all the demonstrators burned their work

---

### The Human Cost of Public Law 78

*In* La Raza: The Mexican Americans, *author Stan Steiner paints a chilling portrait of the effects of the bracero program.*

"Braceros had been herded like cattle. They had no rights, no protection, under our laws. They were not citizens and could not join unions. One word of protest and they could be deported at whim. . . . The bracero system, like that of slavery, was designed to isolate a man from his family, in a strange country, so that he had nothing but his work. . . . The medical files of 'the bracero doctor,' Dr. Ben Yellen, of the Imperial Valley, one of the rare physicians in the farm counties who treat mostly agricultural workers, are a nightmare of illnesses and deaths. . . . None of this misery by itself would have brought an end to the Bracero Law. It was too useful in the fields, and it rendered union organizing impossible."

cards in what Peter Matthiessen called "a gesture of contempt for the corruption of the hiring program."[17] Chavez made sure that the press was invited to the fire.

## A Promising Foundation

Bit by patient bit, Chavez put together an effective farm worker organization, with eighteen hundred members and a reputation for bold action. The growers were nervous: all this "rabble-rousing" might lead to an official investigation of their hiring practices, and nobody wanted that. It was easier to hire domestic workers than to risk a confrontation with the govern-

*Chavez was instrumental in setting up hiring halls where workers could look for jobs and growers could hire workers.*

ment over the terms and provisions of Public Law 78. Before Chavez quite knew what was happening, his CSO office was a bustling center where workers came looking for jobs and growers called to hire whole crews of domestic workers at a single stroke.

Many of the growers came to like the system; it was straightforward and simple. They never had to worry about crops rotting in the field for lack of people to do the picking; best of all, the system was entirely legal. In addition, it was so effective that Chavez did not have to settle for the lowest wages and the worst working conditions. He could dicker for more and have a good chance of getting it.

The implications of the power Chavez now held were staggering: somewhere along the line, the crusade against the abuse of Public Law 78 had become the foundation of a successful farm workers union. Chavez wanted to build on that foundation, but CSO was not interested in labor organizing; that was a job better left to the experts in the AFL-CIO, the umbrella group formed from the merger of the American Federation of Labor and the Congress of Industrial Organizations.

Chavez did not agree; in his mind, union organizing was a natural extension of CSO's political and social agenda. When he pressed the point by citing what fifteen months of work had accomplished in Oxnard, the board reassigned him to the main office in Los Angeles. Though he was promoted to national field director in 1958, the move left him discontented and restless.

Back in Oxnard, the packinghouse workers union of AFL-CIO tried to take over where Chavez had left off, but the hard-nosed, trade union methods that

## Mexican-American Activism

*In their ethnographic study,* Mexican Americans, *Joan W. Moore and Harry Pachon describe how the activism of groups like CSO took an openly political turn in the years after World War II.*

"Toward the end of the 1950s a different type of political organization appeared. The Mexican American Political Association (MAPA) was created in 1959 after the defeat of Mexican American candidates in a California election. . . . The formation of MAPA was closely followed by an event of special significance to the community. The *Viva Kennedy* campaigns were designed expressly to bring out the Latin vote for John Kennedy in the 1960 presidential election. These campaigns drew together Mexican Americans from different states and different organizations. Because the Mexican American was crucial to Kennedy in carrying such states as Texas . . . Mexican Americans received political aid and patronage positions in the early 1960s."

worked in the factories were useless in the fields. The organization fell apart. It was Sal Si Puedes all over again, only worse. This time Chavez did not go back to repair the damage.

## The Same Old Dream

The work in Los Angeles was challenging and productive. As the 1960 presidential elections approached, voter registration drives were more important than ever. During the summer of 1960, CSO registered 137,000 voters. In principle, the registration drive was nonpartisan. In practice, the barrios had always been heavily Democratic; 95 percent of the new voters cast their ballots for John Fitzgerald Kennedy.

When the election was over, Chavez hoped to change the focus of CSO energies from registering voters to organizing workers. It was the same old dream, stronger than ever, because the collapse of all he had done in Oxnard continued to haunt him. He found at least some support for his ideas within the CSO structure, most notably from his mentor Fred Ross, and a fellow Ross protegée named Dolores Huerta.

Huerta was quick-witted and often fiery, with a strong sense of mission and a talent for inspiring people to help themselves. She had set aside a promising teaching career to work with CSO because she believed in what the organization was doing in the barrios and migrant camps of California.

As the daughter of farm workers, Huerta was no stranger to hard work, or to the bleakness of unremitting poverty. At the age of fourteen, she took an after-school job in the Stockton, California, packing sheds, to help with family expenses. Through perseverance and an inborn stubbornness worthy of Chavez himself, Huerta not only finished high school but became the first in her family to earn a college degree.

Huerta met Chavez briefly in 1955, though at that time she saw no hint of the charismatic leader he would become. She told Peter Matthiessen:

> I had heard a lot about him from Fred Ross—Cesar this and Cesar that—but I didn't really get a chance to talk to him the first time I met him, and he didn't make much of an impression on me. I forgot his face. I knew he was a great organizer, but he never showed it; it came out in the reports. He was very unassuming, you see—did a lot of work but never took any leadership role. The first time I really heard him speak was at a board meeting in Stockton in 1957; he had to respond to sharp questions from an attorney, and I was very impressed by the way he handled it.[18]

With people like Dolores Huerta to share his vision, Chavez clung to the hope that he could establish a union for farm workers within the structure of CSO.

## The Hidden Costs of Success

As time passed, the organization gained prominence and a measure of prosperity. The grassroots warmth of house meetings and personal involvement gave way to middle-class respectability that Chavez did not like at all. Staff expense accounts grew fatter, and CSO membership became a status symbol for politicians and professionals. At the same time, meetings that once occurred in homey barrio halls were moved to hotel convention rooms; ordinary farm workers couldn't afford to attend.

As a protest, Chavez refused all salary increases and began showing up at meetings tieless and often unshaven. As he told Peter Matthiessen:

> There were certain rules I set myself as an organizer, and I had to obey them. To come in a new car to organize a community of poor people—that doesn't work. And if you have money, but dress like they do, then it's phony. . . . You can be hungry and have money in the bank, or you can be hungry and have nowhere to go. There's a big difference.[19]

Chavez never lost sight of that difference. To him, suffering and sacrifice were part of leadership, just as aguante was part of human courage. He absorbed this thinking from the teachings of his Catholic faith and the example of the devout Hindu Gandhi, who transformed voluntary poverty and self-sacrifice into a powerful tool for social and political reform. A few months after Chavez's death, journalist Frank Bardacke offered this analysis:

> Cesar Chavez was essentially a lay Catholic leader. . . . What many of the liberals and radicals on the staff [of the United Farm Workers] could never understand was that all of the fasts, the long marches, the insistence on personal sacrifice and the flirting with

## A Friend and Kindred Spirit

*In 1990, on the occasion of Dolores Huerta's sixtieth birthday, her friend and coworker Luis Valdez wrote a moving tribute, published in* Image, *to the woman who helped Cesar Chavez to establish the United Farm Workers.*

"When I think of Dolores Huerta, I think of the Earth. Powerful, beautiful, fecund, challenging, conscious, yet so incredibly delicate. The patina of my superimposed memories of her over the last 25 years glows with dissolving moving images: Dolores as picket captain, Dolores as single mother, Dolores as negotiator, lobbyist, speaker, La Pasionaria de Delano; Dolores as my leader, for she was the first woman general I met and followed into the fray of *La Causa.* Yet these images all come together to form the simple, inspiring portrait of an enduring friend. . . . [Dolores] led through persuasion and personal example, rather than intimidation. . . . People tend to forget that the 60's were in the sexist dark ages, even in The Movement, as we called it, but Dolores was already way out in front. She was a woman, a Mexican-American, a Chicana cutting a swath of revolutionary action across the torpidity of the San Joaquin Valley."

*Dolores Huerta, a strong voice in the fight for farm workers' rights, became a supportive friend to Chavez.*

sainthood were not only publicity gimmicks, they were the essential Chavez.[20]

Because Chavez experienced his convictions as self-evident truths, there was no need to prove them, and certainly no point in arguing about them. This steadfast faith in his own ideals was at the heart of his uncanny ability to inspire others—and his tendency to dismiss competing viewpoints as unworthy, unworkable, and fundamentally wrong.

## Time for Taking a Stand

The breach between CSO and its national director grew wider and more painful in the two years following the Kennedy election. In Washington, a new young president was inspiring the nation, and Congress crept ever closer to a reevaluation of Public Law 78. According to University of Wisconsin professor Joan W. Moore and coauthor Harry Pachon:

> By 1960, sentiment against both Mexican immigrants and Mexican contract laborers had hardened considerably. Congress listened more attentively to labor interests. . . . The long decline of agricultural power in the Border States meant that agriculture no longer dominated legislative opinion.[21]

In other words, southwestern growers were in danger of losing their ability to control both braceros and domestic workers by pitting one against the other. When that happened Chavez wanted to be ready to take advantage of the situation, and that meant having a functioning union in place and ready to move. Everything inside him said it was time to start building such a union, and he was determined to follow that hunch. He became impatient with CSO for its lack of vision and annoyed with himself for his failure to get the point across.

After a great deal of soul-searching, he decided what to do and when to do it. In March 1962, CSO would hold its annual convention in the southern California border town of Calexico; it was there that Chavez would make his move.

# 4  A New Direction

Chavez prepared for the CSO meeting the way a lawyer prepares for court—careful of every fact and detail. He made certain that supporters like Fred Ross and Dolores Huerta were on hand to add their voices to his own. By 1962, after ten years in CSO, the shy, soft-spoken farm worker had become a skilled speaker. He used all that skill in presenting his plea for CSO to get involved in union organizing. When he finished, a low hum went through the room as people discussed the merits of his plan. A short time later, they voted it down.

Chavez knew then what he had to do; he stood up and spoke two words to the startled crowd: "I resign." People jumped to their feet and started arguing. Chavez walked out of the room.

## Hard Decisions and Quiet Reflections

Fred Ross and Dolores Huerta went with Chavez into Mexicali to get something to eat and discuss the events of the day. By the time the three friends got back to Calexico, a representative of the AFL-CIO was waiting to offer Chavez a job with its affiliate, Agricultural Workers Organizing Committee (AWOC) in Stockton.

To Chavez, the giant AFL-CIO seemed cold and impersonal; the leadership knew labor law and organizational methods, but they lacked the spirit of sacrifice he had admired in the work of Gandhi and Thoreau. The union he envisioned would be founded and sustained as a labor of love. Chavez thanked the representative for his offer, but the answer was no. He went back to his office in Los Angeles, where he finished work in progress and organized the office for his replacement. Then he turned in his keys and left.

Ursula Rios Gutierrez, a staff member who was present when Chavez walked out the door, remembered his leaving as a betrayal. She told author Stan Steiner:

> He left for political reasons. He says we were not interested in farm workers. It's not true! One of our wealthy members offered $50,000 for Cesar to organize his farm workers. . . . I was there when he came in and laid his keys on the desk and said, "You probably read my letter of resignation. I am leaving. Here are the keys." And I said, "Yes, I know." That was that. . . . He walked out![22]

Helen and Cesar Chavez packed their eight children into the car and drove up the coast to Carpinteria Beach. This beautiful stretch of California coastline had always been special to Cesar. He had seen it first as a child, picking tomatoes with his family in nearby Summerland. For several seasons of his migrant childhood, the chance to visit that beach had helped to make the fieldwork bearable.

Cesar no longer had to pick tomatoes in Summerland; now he came to Carpinteria when he needed to think. For six days Helen relaxed, the children played, and Cesar pondered the challenges ahead. By the time the family left the beach, he knew where he would go and what he would do.

## A Sensible Place to Start

The Chavezes moved to Delano. For a number of personal and strategic reasons,

this dusty little California farm town east of Bakersfield was a perfect place to start. In Delano, they would be near Helen's family and Cesar's brother Richard. Cesar knew that the months and years ahead would not be easy; at least here, with family close at hand, his wife and children would not starve.

It was good being close to Richard once again. The brothers had been inseparable since childhood. Even as adults they had traveled together and worked together until Cesar took the CSO job in Los Angeles. During that time of separation, Richard had built a solid life in Delano with a home, a family, and a good job.

Though he was glad to have Cesar close again, as Richard told Peter Matthiessen, he was reluctant to get involved with farm worker issues: "I was a journeyman carpenter by that time, and I had my wife and child. So I didn't want to believe in what he was doing. . . . But way down deep, you see, I believed." Cousin Manuel Chavez was even more reluctant: "When Cesar asked him to join the new association, he flatly refused. 'Neither of us are farm workers any more!' he yelled. 'We got away!'"[23] Finally, Manuel agreed to join Cesar for a month. He never went back.

Delano was a major center for grapes, with thirty-eight thousand acres of vineyards producing thousands of pounds of grapes each season. Because a vineyard requires attention all year long, Delano had a population of *campesinos* (farm workers) with permanent homes and more or less steady jobs. That stability would make the workers easier to organize, and those rows of staked and tended vines would become a dramatic symbol of their struggle: "You can't picket bare ground," Chavez once said. "There's a bad psychological blow in all that emptiness."[24]

The vines of Delano were a living reminder that human beings with scarred hands and silent hopes worked in this place. In spring, the vineyards would be glossy green, and at harvest, heavy with fruit. Come autumn, the entire vineyard would turn to shades of scarlet, gold, and soft, cinnamon brown.

## The Organizer and the Chaplain

In the same month that Cesar Chavez came to live and work in Delano, a young protestant minister named Jim Drake also arrived. He never meant to stay. He had come to Delano for six weeks of training at Migrant Ministry, a church-sponsored outreach organization. As a lifelong Californian, Reverend Drake was familiar with the problems facing migrant workers, but he was skeptical about the idea of forming a union. He looked at Chavez and saw a man with a wife, eight children, and a beat-up station wagon that used too much gas. The would-be organizer was dedicated and obviously sincere, but where would he get the money for such an enormous undertaking?

Jim Drake couldn't answer that question, and Cesar Chavez didn't try. He had turned his whole family's life upside down to do something that needed doing; he

*A Delano farm worker packages grapes for transport from the fields.*

## What Is Chicano?

*During the activism of the 1960s, the term* chicano *came into use to describe Mexican Americans. Gradually, the term lost common usage. Earl Shorris explains the change in terminology in* Latinos: A Biography of the People.

"The chicano generation began in the late 1960s and lasted about six or eight years, dying slowly during the seventies. Nothing remains of it now but a handshake practiced by middle-aged men. Some people still call themselves chicanos, but the definition is vague and the word has lost its fire . . . . Six months before he was killed [in August 1970, journalist] Ruben Salazar wrote a column . . . in which he attempted to define the chicano concept for both Mexican Americans and Anglos. . . . 'A chicano is a Mexican-American with a non-Anglo image of himself. He resents being told Columbus "discovered" America when the chicano's ancestors, the Mayans and the Aztecs, founded highly sophisticated civilizations centuries before Spain financed the Italian explorer's trip to the "New World."

'Chicanos resent also Anglo pronouncements that chicanos are "culturally deprived" or that the fact that they speak Spanish is a "problem" . . . [chicanos] will complain that when the governor dresses up as a Spanish nobleman for the Santa Barbara fiesta he's insulting Mexicans because the Spanish conquered and exploited the Mexicans. It's as if the governor dressed like an English Redcoat for a Fourth of July parade, chicanos say.' "

was not going to let money stand in his way. He started out with $1,200 of his own money—his whole life savings—and set up an office in his garage. In the unrelenting heat of a Delano summer, the garage was so hot that ink melted in the mimeograph machine loaned by Jim Drake, and the air felt like it came from a blast furnace.

Helen got a job picking grapes at the sprawling Sierra Vista Ranch, working long hours in the fields and equally long hours at home; it was her contribution to the fledgling union and she made it without complaint. Many times the family did not have enough to eat, yet Cesar remained stubbornly independent of outsiders and their money. Said Jim Drake:

What impressed us most at the Migrant Ministry was that even though Cesar was desperate, he didn't want our money. He made it clear right from the start that whatever organization he got going would be entirely independent; he didn't want any Teamster money or money from the AFL-CIO or any other money that might compromise him.[25]

Drake himself was so impressed that he did not leave Delano after six weeks, as originally planned. He stayed, though the "union" was only an idea in the mind of a former migrant worker with an eighth-grade education and an almost superhuman dedication to his cause. As a clergyman, Jim Drake was accustomed to making leaps of faith, but not even he could guess where Chavez's idea would lead.

## A Foundation for Action

Chavez had learned during his years with CSO that poor people hesitated to make even the most reasonable demands on their employers. Part of this passivity came from the tradition of aguante—endurance. The rest came from fear of a system the workers did not understand. Chavez quickly learned to avoid words like *union*, *strike*, and *boycott*. He called his organization the National Farm Workers Association (NFWA), and when he talked

An elderly field-worker cuts grapes from a Delano vineyard. Because the vineyards needed tending almost all year long, many of the workers had permanent homes in the area, making it easier for Chavez to organize them into a union.

with workers about it he emphasized community action instead of labor negotiations.

The distinction was more than a tactical ploy; Chavez's first priority was building a strong, financially sound organization with enough clout to influence business and government. Only when NFWA was solid and Public Law 78 had been wiped from the books could NFWA hope to win a strike. Chavez figured that would take at least five years. He had no way of knowing that circumstances would destroy his timetable and force NFWA into a historic confrontation with some of the biggest growers in California.

His first priority was surveying the area to find out what the workers needed and wanted. He began before dawn each morning, and often did not stop until after midnight. Because Helen was working and the older children were in school, Cesar took three-year-old Anthony along on his rounds. "Birdy," as the family called the toddler, learned to amuse himself in the car while his father was busy; he even slept there when Cesar held house meetings late into the night. Up and down California's central valley, the man and his young son became a familiar sight.

Wherever there were crews in the fields, Chavez stopped to talk. He told Stan Steiner:

> I am a listener. . . . People know what they want. And what they don't want. It's a case of staying with them and keeping your ears open and your eyes open. And they tell you! They don't tell you in so many words, but they tell you with their actions. They will not so much spell it out for you. They never have a clear way of doing that. . . . It's

never tangible, but if you listen to it, it comes.[26]

The questions Chavez asked were basic, and so were the answers he received: people needed decent housing and enough food to eat. They needed fair wages and protection from *coyotes*.

## Doing What Needed to Be Done

The organizing was painfully slow. Many people had forgotten how to hope for better conditions, let alone work for them. Others cared only about getting out of the fields. For them, activism was a waste of time. Why fight for change when you planned to leave the fields and find other work at the first opportunity?

Chavez did not condemn those who took the second attitude. He knew how it felt to want out—even how it felt to get out—but he also knew that thousands would never make the break. For one reason or another, they would spend the rest of their working lives moving from camp to camp and farm to farm. These were the people who needed a union most of all.

To reach them, Chavez lived on the edges of starvation: "Talk about being scared," he said. "I had to get dues in order to eat. I suspect some of the members were paying dues [$3.50 a month] because they felt sorry for me." With only ten dues-paying members, Chavez found himself forced into one of the most uncomfortable situations of his life, having to beg for food. "I went to the people and started asking for food. It turned out to be about the best thing I could have done, although at first it's hard on your pride. If people give you their food, they'll give you their hearts."[27]

Chavez signed up many of the people who gave him food, and others he met in the fields. As always, his approach to building a group began on a deeply personal level: getting to know people one by one, organizing house meetings, helping whenever and wherever he could. If a worker had to file a disability claim, Chavez helped with the paperwork and talked to the bureaucrats. He even developed an informal network of attorneys who would take migrants' cases for free. Before long, word got around the barrio—if you are in trouble, go to the house on Kensington Street; Cesar Chavez can help. By September 1962, NFWA had nearly 250 dues-paying members and it was time to hold the first official meeting.

## The Gathering in Fresno

Chavez approached that first NFWA meeting on two levels: as a practical exercise in group action and as a dynamic symbol of the spirit and dignity of the campesino. He had never forgotten his resentment of the elegant convention rooms where CSO held its meetings. For NFWA, he chose the cheapest place he could find in Fresno, an abandoned movie theater on the tattered edges of the barrio.

The next step was finding a unifying symbol for the new union, something that would have meaning for every farm worker who saw it. Manuel Chavez volunteered to design a flag. It should be dramatic, he decided, and have some connection to Mexican culture. It should

also be simple to make—a people's flag, not an artist's flag.

Manuel envisioned an Aztec eagle with its wings spread in triumphant flight. Since, however, he could not manage to draw a decent eagle, he settled for a stylized black figure that was all angles, lines, and blocks. NFWA had its flag. The first one was enormous, big enough to fill the screen of the movie theater. Manuel hung it there and covered it over with paper, to be unveiled at the proper, dramatic moment in the meeting.

On September 30, the people gathered to make impassioned speeches, sing *corridos* (folk ballads), and listen to Señor Cesar Chavez tell them about hope and dignity and all the ways they could work together to make life better for everyone. Then it was time to unveil the flag. Cesar stood proudly on the podium while his cousin pulled away the paper covering.

*Cesar Chavez poses in front of the bold red-and-white NFWA flag emblazoned with a black eagle. Manuel Chavez unveiled the flag at the first NFWA meeting, announcing, "When that eagle flies, the farm workers' problems will be solved!"*

There it was, bold as anything and larger than life; a stylized black eagle against a background of white and red. Someone said it looked "kind of Communist." Someone else thought it was too much like the hated Nazi battle flag of World War II. There was a buzz of talk throughout the hall, growing louder as people tried to express their opinions. Cesar, who was wise enough to know when to stand aside, let everyone have a say.

When the hall echoed with heated discussions, Manuel jumped to his feet: "When that eagle flies," he shouted, "the farm workers' problems will be solved!" For a moment, there was silence in the auditorium. Then people started to applaud; Manuel Chavez and his Aztec eagle had won the day.

## A Portable Constitution

The organizational meeting was a triumph for Cesar Chavez, but it was also the beginning of a period of frantic activity, during which he neglected his wife, his family, and his own health to do the work of NFWA. He continued recruiting and helping members with their problems, but he also applied himself to a formidable task—creating a constitution for the union that was not yet called a union.

He planned to hold a constitutional convention in January 1963, and so he worked tirelessly through the holidays and beyond. He read dozens of constitutions from many different unions, analyzing them to determine their strengths and

*Organizers (from left to right) Dolores Huerta, Antonio Orendain, and Cesar Chavez gather for the first NFWA meeting, held in an abandoned movie theater on the edge of the Fresno barrio.*

weaknesses. Which provisions would apply to migrant farm workers and which would not? Chavez had always known that to succeed, a union for migrants would have to be different from other unions. He told Jacques Levy:

> Because of the mobility of the people, I thought that we would need a very strong, centralized administration, and that we could never have a local as other unions have. We couldn't have any geographical restrictions on employment, and I felt that the Union would have to be so alike everywhere that workers could recognize that it was, in fact, one Union. But we also wanted local say-so for the workers. Finally, we decided to have each ranch have its own ranch committee that would elect its own officers, its own stewards, and take care of its own problems.[28]

Bit by bit, Chavez pounded out the document that would become the foundation of NFWA. He wrote and rewrote, changed concepts and then rewrote again. He was still writing on the day before the meeting, which also happened to be Helen's birthday. When the whole family showed up at the door, loaded down with all the makings of a surprise party, Cesar said hello and then took his papers to Richard's house, where he could work undisturbed. When he got home that night, Helen was in tears; her family had been offended by Cesar's behavior. They took it as a sign that the marriage might be in trouble.

Despite all the crises and the questions, Chavez finished the constitution. On January 20, 1963, it was formally adopted by the membership. The first meeting of the new year ended with a sense of optimism and soaring hope, but that feeling did not last. Chavez had expected some fall-off in enthusiasm, but nothing had prepared him for what happened. By summertime, all but a dozen members had dropped out of the organization.

# 5 The War of the Flowers

During the summer of 1963, that crisis of confidence when everything Chavez had worked for seemed doomed to failure, he received a tempting job offer. The Peace Corps wanted to hire him as director of programs in a four-country region of South America. Chavez turned the offer down. He had chosen his course in life and he meant to follow it. With a core of diehard supporters who shared his dream, he began the long process of rebuilding. Quitting had never been Chavez's style.

## The Importance of Timing

Developments in Washington added new urgency to his work; Congress was finally taking a hard look at the bracero program. In the fifties, two-year renewals of certification had been practically automatic. In the sixties, that began to change. Three members of the House Agriculture Committee submitted a devastating report on the impact of the program:

> The moral implications of [the bill] are shocking. . . . It would literally increase the destitution . . . and the exploitation of 2,300,000 domestic farm workers, who are the poorest of the poor in our nation. It would put the family farm at a further competitive disadvantage. It would increase the strain Public Law 78 has already placed on our national values and prestige.[29]

With rumblings like that from Washington, Chavez knew that the bracero program would not last much longer—and he was determined to have NFWA ready to step into the breach. His goal was in step with the times, but his method of accomplishing it seemed like a throwback to simpler days. He would not use the efficient, businesslike methods of the successful industrial unions. He did what he had always done—helped people whenever and however they needed it most.

"People know what they want. And what they don't want," he had told writer Stan Steiner. He had continued to develop this thought:

> It's a case of staying with them and keeping your ears open and your eyes open. . . . Once you begin to "lead" the people, to force them, then you begin to make mistakes. . . . Once you begin to feel you are really the "leader" then you begin to stop being a real leader. Then a reverse process starts. The "leader" has less and less

## The Story of Abernacio Gonzales

*In the uncertain world of migrant farm workers, the experience of Chavez's friend Manuel Rivera is not unusual. In* La Raza: The Mexican Americans, *Stan Steiner tells of the fate of a young man named Abernacio Gonzales, who worked for thirty-three years without being paid a dime.*

"On the old Montoya Ranch, in the hills to the north of Albuquerque [New Mexico] the boy came looking for a job. It was the summer of 1933. He was then thirteen and he was hired as a ranch hand. . . . In those Depression days he was happy to have any job. He had been convinced, he says, to go on working for 50 cents a day and board. He was a hard worker; the rancher liked him and promised, since he was so young, to put his wages away for him. That way he would have money to live on when he was too old to work. He reluctantly agreed to this. Whenever the boy asked to see his bank account, he was cowed into silence. He was beaten when he tried to leave the remote ranch. The boy grew to be a man, but he was afraid to run away lest he lose the years of promised savings. He was a serf in the middle of the twentieth century in the United States.

One day in 1966 Gonzales fled from the Montoya Ranch. He was forty-six, penniless, a novice in the world. . . . He sued for his thirty-three years of back pay, at 50 cents a day, with 6 percent interest, but obviously no court could repay him for his lost youth and stolen manhood."

time for the people. He depends more upon himself, he begins to play hunches, to play the long shots. He loses his touch with the people.[30]

## Rebuilding the Dream

The earliest members of NFWA were people who shared Chavez's vision of what a farm workers union ought to be. One of the first was a man named Manuel Rivera, who had heard through the barrio grapevine that Chavez could help him deal with a dishonest labor contractor.

Rivera's story was all too familiar. He joined a *coyote's* work crew because he needed to earn money and the *coyote* seemed the surest route to finding work. Rivera did this despite the *coyote's* refusal to discuss his rate of pay. When Rivera asked how much he would be paid for work he had already done, the *coyote* kicked him out of the crew truck and refused to pay him at all. Manuel Rivera came to Chavez after he'd been stranded at the bus depot with his wife and children. They had no money, no home, and no car.

Cesar and Helen took the Riveras in, loaned them a car, and even helped them find a place to live after Manuel had found a job. When the grateful farm worker asked Chavez how much he owed him, the reply was *nada*, nothing. Just help some other farm worker in trouble. This, Manuel Rivera promised to do, and soon afterward he left Delano to follow another harvest. Six months later, he returned.

Chavez had almost forgotten the man who showed up on his doorstep with a fistful of money and a smile. Not only did Rivera pay union dues for all the months he had been away, he recruited more than a hundred new members before he left Delano again. "That spirit was what we were looking for . . . it is our strength," said Chavez.[31]

With dedicated members like Manuel Rivera, Chavez rebuilt the union. By August 1964, it was more than a thousand members strong—and Chavez was determined to keep the dream alive.

## A New Mood in the Land

In January 1965, Congress repealed Public Law 78. While domestic farm workers celebrated, growers predicted everything from inflated prices to disastrous shortages of food. They said that crops would rot in the field for lack of workers to do the picking. None of those things happened.

What did happen was that farm workers on both sides of the border had a freer market for their services. Situations they once accepted in the spirit of *aguantar* were suddenly open to question and even protest. In this new and hopeful climate, Rev. Jim Drake and a former CSO worker named Gilbert Padilla organized a rent strike that would close the infamous Kern-Tulare labor camps. These bleak shantytowns, erected by the federal government during the Great Depression, were never

*This tin shack, which had no heat or running water, was part of hastily constructed government housing for farm laborers during the Great Depression. Chavez's supporters organized a rent strike to close down the grim shantytowns, still in use thirty years after their construction.*

meant for permanent use. Even in the thirties the camps were instant slums; the tin shacks had no heat or running water It was only for a while, the government said, to serve as a refuge for people with nowhere else to go.

By the early forties, the world was at war and able-bodied Americans left the fields of California for the bunkers and the trenches of Europe. In the emergency, the state of California took control of the delapidated camps and used them to house the Mexican braceros who had come because of the labor shortage. After the war, nobody quite got around to dismantling the substandard camps.

Over the next thirty years, the shacks deteriorated but remained in use. When the California Housing Authority announced a rent increase in 1965, the protest began. "The state was making a big profit on those slums," said Jim Drake, "[and] when the workers found out about that profit, it wasn't hard to organize a rent strike."[32]

In the best tradition of nonviolent activism, the tenants refused to pay their rent. They picketed the camps, carrying signs, shouting slogans, making their problem known. When the press and the public began asking questions, the housing authority agreed to tear down the shacks and replace them with decent housing. Chavez was overjoyed. The Kern-Tulare rent strike was more than one small victory in a very large war: It was proof that nonviolence could work in Delano, California, as it had in New Delhi, India, and Montgomery, Alabama. "The rent strike," said Chavez, "was one of the best ways of educating farm workers that there was a Union concerned with their economic interests. It was one of the first

demonstrations when the black eagle flew."[33] It would not be the last.

## Getting Down to Business

A core group was forming around Cesar and his dream. There was the Chavez family, of course—Helen, Manuel, and Richard—and friends like Fred Ross, Rev. Jim Drake, and Dolores Huerta. There was a group of young activists more or less led by Antonio Orendain, a handsome young man who read gloom-and-doom philosophers and took a great deal of pride in his role as resident cynic. NFWA got its first real office—an old grocery store that Cesar and his friends cleaned and painted and proudly furnished. In honor of the occasion, Richard Chavez built a desk for his brother's office. It was made of pinewood and painted red, but to Cesar's eyes it was more beautiful than the finest mahogany or hand-rubbed oak. The National Farm Workers Association was in business, and before long a rose grafter named Epifiano Camacho and two other men came to ask for help.

Rose grafting is a specialized skill. Using a knife sharp as a surgeon's scalpel, the grafter cuts tiny slits into mature rose bushes and inserts live buds. When a graft is successful, the new buds bloom and grow as part of the older bush. The trick is knowing where to place each bud so it will take hold; a wrong placement or an accidental slip of the knife can destroy an entire plant.

A grafter works on his knees, crawling from plant to plant, along the endless rows. His hands bleed from the thorns; over time, his fingers become dark with

*With the help of dedicated volunteers like Antonio Orendain (pictured), Chavez gained the support he needed to make the NFWA a powerful union. Orendain led a group of young activists who publicized NFWA concerns.*

permanent scars. He ignores the scratches just as he ignores anything else that might distract him or break his rhythm. He must work with all possible speed because he is paid on a piecework basis. In 1965 the growers had promised $9.00 per thousand plants, but they did not keep their word. The workers were actually making less than $7.00 per thousand.

Would Chavez be willing to help them? Yes, was the answer. As with the Kern-Tulare rent strike, the grafters' pay was a single, well-defined issue. The grafters themselves had a bargaining chip that most farm workers lacked: a job that required special skills. They would not be easy to replace. With these factors in their favor, NFWA could make an impact with a relatively small investment of time and money.

Chavez got to work right away. Though there were several rose growers in the area, he did not want to spread his forces too thin. He decided to target only one: Mount Arbor Nurseries, the largest grower of roses in California. More than eighty-five grafters worked there.

No one seems to know who dubbed the grafters' strike the "war of the flowers," but the name was a masterstroke. In the minds of people who knew their Mexican history, it connected a 1965 labor dispute with an ancient Aztec ritual. The Aztec War of the Flowers was a mock battle, fought on a ceremonial field. Like a modern football game, it was surrounded by the pageantry of flags and marches and cheering crowds. There the similarity ends, for this was no ordinary game; it was a life or death struggle in which every member of the losing side was sacrificed to the war god Huitzilopochtli. Not even Chavez could have created a more compelling symbol for the urgency of the grafters' struggle.

Like its ancient namesake, this war of the flowers would be a dramatization of reality. Chavez knew he could not hope to win a long strike; there was no time for complex negotiations and agreements that only a lawyer could understand. The grafters needed a grand, symbolic gesture to draw attention to their plight—and Chavez knew exactly what that gesture ought to be.

On the morning of May 3, 1965, exactly at sunrise, Epifiano Camacho got up off his knees and shouted a single word: "Huelga!" ("Strike!"). That was the signal. Everyone stood up, and together the grafters walked away from the field of roses. The strike had begun, and with it the legend of Epifanio Camacho, who soon became known all over California's central valley as "the man who got off his knees."

Overhead in a pale morning sky, the black eagle flew for all the world to see. After that, there was no turning back; something changed when the strikers raised that bold flag. It was a landmark for every farm worker who had dreamed of standing up to his bosses, and for the union that Cesar Chavez had created out of a lifelong dream.

The war of the flowers lasted only a few days. Mount Arbor refused to give the workers a contract that specified their rights, duties, and rate of pay, but did grant a wage increase that lasted for the rest of that season. This hardly qualified as a sweeping victory for Chavez and NFWA, but it was a start—the beginning of a much larger effort to help farm workers get their share of the American dream.

It was also another learning experience in a bad news/good news kind of way. On the positive side, Chavez had learned a great deal about selecting a target, organizing demonstrations, and conducting a labor strike. On the negative side, he had received a hard lesson in the difficulty of inducing poor people to move past breadbasket issues.

He who is hungry thinks only of bread was a dicho like the ones Juana Chavez liked to quote, and Cesar had seen the truth of it firsthand. After all the work of setting up a dramatic beginning to the strike, Dolores Huerta found four workers getting dressed to go to work the next morning. She stopped them by the effective but undiplomatic strategy of blocking their driveway with her truck and hiding the keys to their car.

Chavez was not able to convince the strikers that they needed more than a simple raise in pay; they needed a bona fide labor contract. Without that, nothing they

## A Gift of Flowers

*Flowers were a potent symbol for the McFarland strikers. As John O. West explains in* Mexican-American Folklore, *both European and Aztec traditions used flowers in their death rituals.*

"The custom of paying tribute to the dead is worldwide, and exists in many cultures—the Druids did it on October 31 each year, Asians do it in connection with the Lunar New Year, and of course Catholics have been doing it for centuries. . . . European customs related to All Saints' and All Souls' Days have merged with the practice of the Indians who were here before the Spanish. Flowers, especially white ones for children and yellow for adults, were used by the Aztecs to decorate the graves of their loved ones."

*After organizing Filipino workers to strike against low-paying grape growers, labor activist Larry Itliong called upon Chavez to help get Mexican-American workers involved.*

gained would last beyond a single season. The workers listened politely enough, but as soon as the company agreed to the raise, they voted to return to work without a contract. The union had a long way to go.

## Meeting Larry Itliong

After the war of the flowers, Chavez was more certain than ever that NFWA was not ready for a major strike. He had a dozen solid, serviceable reasons for this opinion but none of them mattered when he met a Filipino with long experience in the labor movement. Larry Itliong had come to the United States in 1929 when he was only fifteen years old. By the time he was sixteen,

he was involved in his first strike. He had been a labor activist ever since.

Itliong's latest accomplishment was a perfectly timed strike by grape pickers in the Coachella Valley. Their organization, the Agricultural Workers Organizing Committee (AWOC), had managed to take the table grape growers by surprise. There on the edge of the Mojave Desert, even a few extra days in the heat could destroy an entire crop. The growers were well aware of that fact. Just ten days into the strike, they raised wages to $1.40 per hour, and the jubilant Filipino pickers went back to work.

A few weeks later the grape harvest began in the Delano area. Some of the same growers who paid $1.40 in Coachella were offering only a dollar an hour in Delano. The Filipino pickers voted to strike. Larry Itliong realized that this would not be another ten-day wonder, and he did not mince words when he told the workers about the difficult road ahead: "If you go out you're going to go hungry, lose your car, maybe lose your wife," he told them.[34] The workers listened, because they respected Larry Itliong, but nothing he said could persuade them to back down. On September 8, 1965, two thousand Filipino workers walked out of the vineyards and Larry Itliong found himself facing the biggest challenge of his career as an organizer. He had to get the Mexican-American workers involved, or the growers would use them to break the strike. He went straight to the NFWA office to talk with its charismatic founder, Cesar Chavez.

# 6 No Turning Back

The news of the AWOC strike placed Chavez in a quandary. Though he felt a moral obligation to support the Filipino grape pickers, he did not think NFWA was ready to mount a full-scale strike. There was no money to keep the workers going while they were unemployed, no money for rallies and picket lines, no money for anything. Would NFWA be strong enough to face those odds? Chavez did not know.

There was also another concern, one that he did not even like to think about. His group was mostly Mexican American, while the AWOC membership was Filipino. The members came from different regions of the world, spoke different languages, even ate different food. Aside from poverty and farm work, all they shared was being from countries where the majority of people had black hair and bronze skin, and belonged to the Roman Catholic Church. Could they work together for a common cause?

The question pointed toward the kind of racism and bigotry Chavez detested. It made him remember his childhood, when cafes had signs that said "No dogs or Mexicans allowed," and children were punished for speaking Spanish in school. He had made up his mind a long time ago not to judge anybody by skin color or eye shape. As long as he was leader of the union, race prejudice would not be allowed.

Chavez had studied enough history to realize that the growers' tactic of pitting one group of workers against another did not begin or end with the bracero program. For decades, this ploy had prevented farm workers from uniting to demand better wages and more humane working conditions. Challenging that institutionalized bigotry would not be easy, but Chavez was determined to try. He would start with the Filipino workers in AWOC.

## Toward a New Unity

Filipinos began coming to the United States during the 1920s. It was boom time in America; World War I was over, and the country was more prosperous than ever before. Farm workers quit the fields for better-paying industrial jobs, leaving California growers with chronic labor shortages. To solve this problem the growers sent professional recruiters to the Philippines, to sign up young, single men who would come to work as agricultural laborers. That arrangement lasted until the Great Depression put a rude end to

## Joining Forces

*In* La Raza: The Mexican Americans, *Stan Steiner first quotes a young Filipino woman who tells about the begining of the strike, then continues, describing the situation that faced Chavez and Larry Itliong.*

" 'It was the young Filipino boys that started the strike. These young boys have a lot of violence inside of them, and when they had a picket line at the field all of the workers left. Most of these boys left when it was decided that there could be no violence on the picket line. But these Filipino boys started the strike. And if it wasn't for them, the old men never would have left the field and joined the strike.'

With the grapes rotting on the vines, growers begin to hire scabs, mostly Mexicans. The farm workers are divided. Not merely do they speak different languages, but they belong to different groups. In the AWOC of Itliong are the Filipinos, and in the NFWA of Chavez are the Mexicans. Itliong goes to Chavez for help. Both men know that if they do not get together, the strike will be lost."

America's decade-long spending spree. In the hardscrabble thirties so many people were out of work and desperate that there was an oversupply of farm labor—and the Filipinos became expendable.

The government imposed immigration quotas and even offered free passage home to Filipinos already living in the United States. Many accepted the offer, leaving behind a group that was desperately poor and unconnected to the surrounding culture. Like other migrants, they survived by working for starvation wages. In a labor market with a hundred workers for every ten jobs, competition was fierce and feelings ran high. To growers, who were having their own financial difficulties in the crumbling economy, the oversupply of labor was a godsend; it kept wages low and workers submissive. If one group was foolish enough to strike, another would be there to take its place in the fields.

Chavez had lived through those depression years, and the bracero years besides. Even in the social upheavals of the sixties, farm workers faced the same old problems: They were disorganized, unskilled—and replaceable. No matter how he looked at the present situation, Chavez could think of a dozen reasons why he should *not* call a strike, but only one reason why he should: It was the right thing to do. To his way of thinking, that was enough.

Once Chavez decided to support AWOC, he went about it with his usual dogged determination. He called a board meeting to discuss the situation and plan a strategy: "We decided to drop everything and start organizing for a mass meeting to get a good strike vote," he told Jacques Levy. "I wanted to have the meeting on September 16, Mexican Independence Day, the great Mexican holiday marking the end of Spanish rule. There was much to do, finding a meeting place, getting all the members there, and preparing a case for us with the growers, AWOC, and the public."[35]

For the meeting, Chavez wanted more than a large auditorium; he wanted a place that would be rich in symbolic meaning. He chose the hall at Our Lady of Guadalupe Church in Delano, where the largely Roman Catholic membership would feel both comfortable and inspired. Working feverishly, Chavez and the board members prepared the hall, hanging the enormous black eagle flag that Manuel Chavez had made, along with signs, slogans, and a picture of Mexican revolutionary hero Emiliano Zapata.

On September 16, 1965, the parish hall was packed. A band played Mexican songs and people talked and laughed and visited as if they had nothing to do but celebrate the independence of their ancestral homeland. Underneath that high-spirited fiesta atmosphere, there was an unmistakable current of determination. Here and there members of a small group would raise their voices in what was to become the watchword of the movement: "Viva la causa!" ("Long live the cause!"). For Chavez, this was a magical moment; he let the people celebrate, let them speak their minds. Then he took the podium:

A hundred and fifty-five years ago in the state of Guanajuato in Mexico, a padre proclaimed the struggle for liberty. He was killed, but ten years later Mexico won its independence. . . . We are engaged in another struggle for the freedom and dignity which poverty denies us. But it must not be a violent struggle, even if violence is used against us. Violence can only hurt us and our cause. . . . The strike was begun by the Filipinos, but it is not exclusively for them. . . . Tonight we must decide if we are to join our fellow workers in this great labor struggle.[36]

The vote, when it came, was unanimous: NFWA would strike. Once more, the cry "Huelga!" echoed in Chavez's ears. Before the meeting ended, the membership reaffirmed a commitment to nonviolence and voted to bring their wage demands

*A strong proponent of change through peaceful means, Chavez told the AWOC and NFWA members, "Violence can only hurt us and our cause."*

into line with those of the Filipino pickers. If everybody was asking $1.40 an hour, it would be harder for the growers to play one group against the other.

## Huelga!

Although *huelga* translates into English as "strike," its meaning in Spanish is not exactly the same according to Cesar Chavez's friend Luis Valdez, a man with a poet's sensitivity to both languages:

> *Strike* is a cruel word that means "to lash out, to attack.". . . In the Spanish the meaning is different. The old word, *huelga*, meant a time of rest and relaxation and merry-making—a little fiesta. The new word *huelga* is more vigorous and joyous still . . . the Delano grape strikers have made it mean a dozen other things. It is a declaration, a challenge, a greeting, a feeling, a movement. . . . It is the most significant word in our entire Mexican American history.[37]

Chavez was buoyed by the spirit of the Independence Day meeting, but that did not mean he wanted to charge into the fray without first offering to talk with the growers. Experience had taught him that the effort would be useless, but he felt duty-bound to give it a try. He sent registered letters to all the growers, asking to meet. He had Dolores Huerta and Jim Drake call them on the telephone, and even asked the mayor of Delano to arrange a meeting at city hall. Nothing worked. The letters came back unopened, nobody would talk to Huerta or Reverend Drake, and the mayor, who did suggest the meeting, practically got impeached for such a foolish idea.

The strike began on September 20, 1965, when eleven hundred NFWA members walked off the job. Chavez plunged into the task of lining up volunteers and

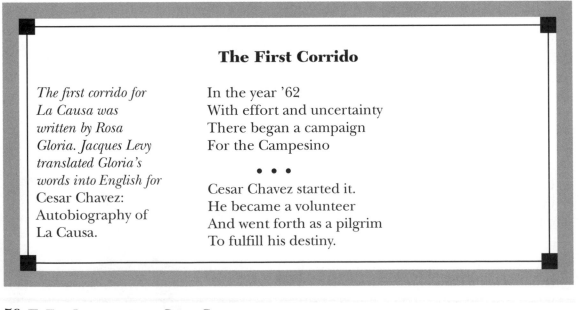

### The First Corrido

*The first corrido for La Causa was written by Rosa Gloria. Jacques Levy translated Gloria's words into English for* Cesar Chavez: Autobiography of La Causa.

In the year '62
With effort and uncertainty
There began a campaign
For the Campesino

• • •

Cesar Chavez started it.
He became a volunteer
And went forth as a pilgrim
To fulfill his destiny.

*Protesters, armed with signs and a bullhorn, picket California grape growers.*

financial aid. He spoke at colleges and universities, made personal appeals to the local clergy and to civil rights organizations such as the Student Nonviolent Coordinating Committee (SNCC) and the Congress of Racial Equality (CORE). The results of these contacts were mixed; most of the clergy denounced him, fearing that his workers movement was tainted by "Godless communism." Even the local chapter of CSO came out against the strike, though that stand was quickly repudiated by the national organization. It turned out that the leader of Delano's CSO had a reason for defending the status quo: he worked part time as a farm labor contractor.

Making speeches before large audiences was not one of Chavez's favorite things. He considered himself a listener, not a speaker. Commitment, along with a generous dash of the famous Chavez stubbornness, carried him through the ordeal. He was often heckled or called insulting names, and sometimes matters threatened to get out of hand, as Peter Matthiessen reports:

> Once [Chavez] was pelted with eggs and tomatoes, but by this time he was so exhausted that he scarcely noticed.

He kept right on with his speech. Apparently, his inert manner was taken for beautiful cool, because the booing changed to wild applause, which he scarcely noticed, either; he just kept droning away.[38]

## Building a Peaceable Army

With time and patience, Chavez recruited a group of young activists who shared his belief in La Causa. Many were veterans of the civil rights movement and opponents of the war in Vietnam, wise in the ways of nonviolent social action. They could teach the farm workers. Their classroom would be the picket line, where strikers might face anything from simple heckling to official harassment or even physical assault.

Some of Chavez's closest advisers thought the volunteers would create as many problems as they solved, bringing their own agendas into La Causa. Chavez did not agree:

Of course, there were problems. When we started the strike . . . some of the volunteers were for ending the Vietnam war above all else, and that shocked the workers because they thought that was unpatriotic. Once, when there was a group more interested in ending the war, I let them have a session with the farm workers. After a real battle, the volunteers come to me astounded. "But they support the war!" they said. "How come?" I told them farm workers are ordinary people, not saints.[39]

As usual, Chavez listened to everyone's opinions, then did what he thought was right. The result was a mixture of races, cultures, and religious persuasions that thrived on its own diversity. Most volunteers came in, did what they could, and

*Strikers brandish signs bearing the black eagle of the NFWA. The strike brought together people of all ages, races, and religions.*

## An Equal Opportunity Union

*Chavez's stand against racism in all its forms was always firm. While Peter Matthiessen was working on* Sal Si Puedes, *he watched Chavez talking with a multiracial group of high school students.*

"Chavez talked to them about race prejudice and the problems he had in his own union. . . . 'The *chicanos* wanted to swing against the Filipinos. We don't permit that against anyone. I told them they'd have to get somebody else to run the union. You don't take a vote on those things, whether to discriminate or not. You don't ask people whether they want to do that or not—you just don't do it.'

In his audience, the black, white and brown students were quiet. He regarded them. 'That doesn't mean you can't be proud of what you are. In the Union we're just beginning, and you're just beginning. . . . Mexican-American youth is just beginning to wake up.'"

*Young people cheer as Chavez speaks about his goals for the union. Chavez spoke with disdain of race prejudice but told students, "That doesn't mean you can't be proud of what you are."*

went on their way; a few came and stayed. People like Luis Valdez and Marshall Ganz brought new dimensions to La Causa, and became supportive friends to Chavez.

Ganz was a rabbi's son with a passionate commitment to social justice. He had dropped out of Harvard University to go south, where he became the only white civil rights organizer in Macombe County, Mississippi. It was dangerous work, and having faced that danger, Marshall Ganz would not be easily intimidated by growers, politicians, or bureaucrats. This fearlessness, along with a gift for strategy, soon made him an invaluable ally in the struggle for farm workers' rights.

Luis Valdez was a Mexican American who had escaped the barrio to get a university education, which was supposed to earn him a place in the middle class. Like many minority youth of the time, he felt out of place in a predominantly Anglo world. He was homesick for Mexican people and Mexican places, so he went to Delano to spend a few weeks working for La Causa. He stayed to organize a farm workers' theater group, *Teatro Campesino*. The actors were all farm workers; the sets, props, and costumes patched together from castoffs. It was homegrown theater, earthy and compelling. Performances not only enlivened Friday night union meetings, but presented the NFWA message to people who otherwise might not have heard it at all. Chavez was thrilled; like the songs, the slogans, and the black eagle flag, Teatro Campesino expressed the undying spirit of the people.

*Marshall Ganz (far left) with UFW officials. Ganz brought to La Causa a passionate commitment to social justice.*

## Targeting the Strikebreakers

That spirit had to be strong in order to deal with strikebreakers. Chavez had learned all about them when he was a little boy on the migrant circuit. *Scabs* they were called, and people did not just say the word—they snarled it. If growers had enough scabs to harvest their fields, they would not negotiate with the union. Chavez knew he had to deal with the problem straightaway. He would never allow violence, but he had nothing against harsh words or public demonstrations. He gladly used the work of American writer Jack London, a veteran of depression-era labor struggles. The union newsletter printed London's famous definition of a scab:

*Luis Valdez (above) organized a farm workers' theater group to present the NFWA message to a wide variety of people through performances. Chavez and Jim Drake (right) enjoy a production by the Teatro Campesino in Delano, California.*

After God had finished the rattlesnake, the toad and the vampire, he had some awful substance left with which he made a Strikebreaker. A Strikebreaker is a two-legged animal with a corkscrew soul, a waterlogged brain, and a combination backbone made of jelly and glue. Where others have hearts, he carries a tumor of rotten principles. . . . Esau was a traitor to himself, Judas Iscariot was a traitor to his God. Benedict Arnold was a traitor to his country. A Strikebreaker is a traitor to himself, a traitor to his God, a traitor to his country, a traitor to his family and a traitor to his class. There is nothing lower than a Strikebreaker.[40]

Chavez believed that going after the so-called scabs was the best way to get the growers. "We knew every place [the strikebreakers] went," he told Jacques Levy, "and we would just keep after them day and night. We'd get a lot of them to leave, and we would convert a lot of them. Those who weren't converted were immobilized because of the constant pressure.[41]

That pressure was never violent, but it was hard-hitting and very direct:

We would take five hundred people and go have a pray-in or a sing-in in front of their homes, or we would put two or three pickets with A Scab Lives Here signs to parade up and down the street. . . . We would distribute leaflets and put on very simple plays depicting the scabs as something awful. We just put as much pressure as we could, and it worked. Some just quit.[42]

The strategy was simple; every strikebreaker who left the field represented a loss of time and money to the grower. As Chavez explained to Jacques Levy:

Somebody else may take their place or it looks like the job is filled, but it isn't really. There's a loss of time. The grower is getting people who are not experienced, who have never seen grapes in their lives . . . that's a loss of money. We've got to make the grower spend fifty dollars to our one dollar. . . . We affect production and costs and profit. And if we hold out, we can win.[43]

# 7 Baptisms of Fire

By the winter of 1965 the grape strike was beginning to take hold, but still the growers refused to talk or even acknowledge the union's right to existence. There was tension in the streets of Delano as strikers, strikebreakers, growers, and police began confronting one another and taking sides. Chavez worked harder than ever to maintain peace on the picket lines and to get the workers' message to the growers, the government, and the general public.

The growers were furious. They were not accustomed to this kind of rebellion and they meant to put it down hard and fast, before other migrant workers got any ideas. On the very first day of the strike, Chavez sent two men to picket at the front gate of a large ranch. They took up positions and raised their signs so motorists on the road and strikebreakers in the field could see them. The next thing they knew, a red-faced, screaming man brandished a shotgun in their faces, grabbed the signs, and set them on fire. The police did not arrest the man, or even question him about the incident. Chavez knew then that his fledgling union was going to be tested to the very limits of its endurance.

A few days later, a group of half-drunk growers left a party they were attending to attack pickets in front of a labor contractor's home. By the time Chavez got there,

one picket had been beaten; the rest were bruised and shaken, but still walking up and down in front of the *coyote's* house. Chavez picked up a sign and joined them. The growers plowed through the line like

*From atop a car, a striker waves the NFWA flag. As time passed and the grape strike produced no results, tension among strikers, strikebreakers, and growers mounted.*

so many bowling balls, knocking pickets to the ground, sometimes giving them a knee or an elbow.

The Filipino pickers were having a union meeting when they got word of the disturbance. Without hesitation, they piled into cars and rushed to the aid of their brothers. The growers were soon surrounded by angry crowds of farm workers. The police broke up the confrontation but arrested only one grower—a man who had made the mistake of attacking a uniformed officer.

During these days of nearly unchecked violence in Delano, an enraged salesman named Lowell Jordan Schy jumped into a truck, shoved it into gear, and ran over a picketing worker. According to a civil complaint, Schy "did maliciously, deliberately, and willfully assault and batter plaintiff by driving a flatbed truck, California license number W49-554, over plaintiff's body. . . ."[44]

The injured worker was Manuel Rivera, the man who had recruited a hundred new members to thank Chavez for helping him and his family after a labor contractor had left them stranded at the Delano bus depot. Chavez had a special place in his heart for this courageous and loyal friend, yet he found himself in the uncomfortable position of protecting the assailant.

When the workers saw Rivera lying on the ground, bleeding and still, they went after Schy. Chavez made his way through the pressing crowd and climbed on the running board of the truck that had just run down his friend. The strikers booed when he called for nonviolence. They were no longer interested in noble philosophies; the time for talk had passed. They wanted blood.

Chavez stood his ground; if the crowd wanted Lowell Schy, they would have to go through their leader to get him. That, nobody was willing to do. Screams turned to low-voiced grumbling as Chavez led the trembling assailant to safety. Manuel Rivera survived, but the assault left him crippled for life. Schy was never arrested.

In the weeks that followed, nonunion pickers continued to work in the fields and growers continued to threaten and harass the strikers. The police took no action, except to follow Chavez and keep the union offices under twenty-four-hour surveillance. After a few weeks of this sort of tension, Chavez realized that picketing the fields was not enough. To draw the widespread attention this strike needed, NFWA would have to do more than picket the fields. They would have to go after the harvested grapes.

## The First Boycott

When Delano grapes arrived at the docks in San Francisco in December 1965, Chavez was there with a group of union members. He set up a picket line at one of the piers, and the longshoremen who would have loaded the cargo ships walked off the job. They were members of the International Longshoremen's and Warehousemen's Union (ILWU) and they would not cross another union's picket line. The growers back in Delano were frantic. Al Green, who was the AFL-CIO liaison for AWOC, was furious with Chavez. As an old-time labor organizer Green believed there was a right way and a wrong way to do things—picketing on the docks was the wrong way. NFWA's fight was with

## A Look at Delano

*In* Mexican Americans, *coauthored with Harry Pachon, Joan W. Moore discussed Chavez's impact on Delano and other small farming towns.*

"Many of these communities seem to have been completely bypassed by the enormous growth and expansion of California. Here the local elite are the large agricultural growers. Oddly and significantly, many of the growers are relative newcomers to the United States themselves. In Delano, the focus of a protracted and bitter agricultural strike, the growers are largely Slavic and Italian immigrants who are quite new to this kind of entrepreneurship. But whatever their personal status, the new and old large-scale employers of Mexican agricultural labor feel themselves threatened and embattled by Cesar Chavez' attempts to organize agricultural workers, something which has never been successful in the past. Some employers attempt to play a paternal role and to help their laborers settle and accept some of the public opportunities available in California. But even more of them simply assume the present inferiority of their Mexican help. In this respect the power structure of these communities (Delano is only one among them) is little changed from the California agricultural community of a generation ago."

the growers in Delano, not the shipping lines in San Francisco. Green demanded that the pickets leave the docks immediately.

"He was so angry he cussed me," Chavez told Jacques Levy, "and I cussed him back. In fact, I not only cussed him back, I went at him on the phone, really tore him up. I was so mad he finally realized it and pulled back."[45] It was one of the few times that the usually soft-spoken Chavez lashed out at anyone. The argument with Al Green did not really end after the NFWA leader's outburst; it simply stopped, to be continued at another time. The longshoremen went back to work, Chavez and his people went back to Delano to plan their next move, and Al Green went back to his offices to prepare for the upcoming AFL-CIO annual convention in San Francisco.

Chavez had read about the power of the economic boycott when he began to pursue his dream of a union for farm workers; in San Francisco, he had seen that power for himself. With a few untrained but dedicated people, the tiny NFWA had stopped three cargo ships

*Chavez's message was heard nationwide. Here, protesters in Albany, New York, picket grape and lettuce growers.*

from transporting Delano grapes to overseas markets. He decided that a tightly focused effort would have the best chance of success, and so he directed the boycott at one company: Schenley Wines, biggest user of grapes in the Delano area.

The tactic succeeded beyond his wildest dreams. By the end of the year, the grandson of writer Jack London had led a picket line on the San Francisco docks, newspapers and television stations had sent reporters to find out what was happening, and the boycott had spread all the way to New York's Harlem, where 95 percent of the predominantly African-American residents said no to Schenley wines.

## Help from Outside the Union

Keeping up the pressure took a toll on union resources; it was all Chavez could

do to keep the strike going, let alone the boycott. By December 1965, he was nearing desperation; member dues and small contributions were simply not enough to pay for everything. Then Walter Reuther, president of the United Auto Workers (UAW), came to see for himself what was happening in Delano. Like Al Green, Reuther was from the old school of labor organizing; it was a matter of principle and policy for established unions to help new ones get started. Reuther took that policy seriously, pledging $5,000 per month for NFWA for the duration of the strike and an equal amount for AWOC.

Even with Reuther's generosity, Chavez had to go on a fund-raising tour to get his people through the long winter. While he was gone, morale sank to an all-time low. Richard Chavez worried that all the volunteers would quit before his brother got back to town. On an impulse, he used union funds to take the staff for beers at their favorite hangout.

When Cesar found out he was furious. The deeper he went into union work, the stricter he became. He gave up smoking and drinking, not because he thought they were wrong or unhealthy, but because they wasted time and money. At the office, he cut down on anything he saw as unnecessary, from making too many phone calls to reading a newspaper at work. He did not intend to punish people, nor did he mean to make them unhappy; he just wanted everyone to share his complete dedication to the task at hand.

The boycott had done more than cost Schenley Wines a great deal of money; it had attracted attention in Washington, D.C. The Senate Subcommittee on Migratory Labor had scheduled hearings in Delano on March 16, 1966. Senator Robert Kennedy would be there to listen to testimony and evaluate the migrant labor situation. Chavez knew, however, that not even Kennedy's support could right all the farm workers' wrongs.

There was still work to be done; the hearings would focus national attention on the farm workers' plight. To take full advantage of that attention, Chavez began looking for a grand gesture that would keep people thinking about La Causa after the hearings were over. He decided on a march.

## The Long March

The idea grew naturally, rooted in the time-honored tradition of *peregrinación* (pilgrimage). In Mexico during the Lenten season, which precedes Easter, faithful Catholics often made such journeys as a sign of penitence for their sins. Chavez did not hesitate to draw upon this tradition; the farm workers' march would be a true pilgrimage. Its theme would be "penitence, pilgrimage, and revolution" and the banner of the Virgin of Guadalupe would lead the way.

### The Hearings in Delano

*When the Senate Subcommittee on Migratory Labor decided to convene in California, Chavez made sure they came to Delano. In* Sal Si Puedes, *Peter Matthiessen reports on the inquiry that ensued.*

"The chairman of the committee was Democratic Senator Harrison A. Williams, Jr., of New Jersey, who had been the farm workers' best friend in Congress since 1959, when the subcommittee was established. 'Any thoughtful person,' Senator Williams has said, 'who observes the poverty and total wretchedness of the lives of migratory farm workers and their youngsters will never leave the work of trying to improve these lives until it is done.' In the course of the hearings, the strikers were blessed with the unanimous support of the seven Catholic bishops of California."

Not everybody agreed with Chavez's Roman Catholic emphasis: Luis Valdez was a nonbeliever, Marshall Ganz was Jewish, and Epifiano Camacho, "the man who got up off his knees" in the war of the flowers, was Protestant. Al Green, the AFL-CIO liaison for AWOC, thought religious symbolism was out of line in a labor demonstration. None of them could get Chavez to budge. Camacho was supposed to be captain of the march, in honor of his role in the McFarland strike against Mount Arbor Nurseries. He withdrew

*With the banner of the Virgin of Guadalupe between the U.S. and Mexican flags, marchers begin their pilgrimage to draw national attention to La Causa.*

rather than follow a banner of a denomination that was not his own.

On March 17, 1966, the day after the hearings, the pilgrimage began. A color guard led the procession, carrying the banner of the Virgin and the black eagle of NFWA, along with the American and Mexican flags. When Larry Itliong and the Filipino workers joined the march over Al Green's objections, the AWOC flag took its place beside the black eagle. The flags carried a silent, simple message to everyone who saw them: Farm workers marched for God, country, and one another, and they would not be turned aside. The Virgin's banner had a particularly powerful effect, wrote Luis Valdez:

> The Virgin of Guadalupe was the first hint to farm workers that the pilgrimage implied social revolution. During the Mexican Revolution, the peasant armies of Emiliano Zapata carried her standard, not only because they sought her divine protection, but because she symbolized the Mexico of the poor and humble. It was a simple Mexican Indian, Juan Diego, who first saw her in a vision at Guadalupe. Beautifully dark and Indian in feature . . . she is a Catholic saint of Indian creation—a Mexican.[46]

## Everybody Get Together

At every stopover, the marchers invited local farm workers to an evening of singing, speeches, and performances by the Teatro Campesino. In the town of Porterville, local supporters spontaneously came up with another way to involve people in the work of La Causa. Chavez told Jacques Levy:

*At a stopover on the march, members of the Teatro Campesino perform a skit to recount the struggles of farm workers.*

Maybe a couple hundred farm workers met us at the entrance of town. They brought their guitars and accordions, and we marched, singing, through town to the park. At the meeting that night . . . the local people asked if they could march with us the next day and act as standard-bearers, carrying the big flags at the head of the march. Of course we thought it was a tremendous idea, and we incorporated that for the rest of the march. At each meeting, we persuaded people to assume the responsibility of carrying the standards for the next day's march.[47]

Chavez's feet got so blistered that he could barely walk, and still he pushed on, using a cane when he had to, riding when his doctors insisted. He refused to take any painkillers; this journey was, after all, an act of penitence and contrition. It was not supposed to be comfortable.

By the time the march arrived in Fresno, Chavez's feet were mostly healed.

The Anglo mayor of this central valley town hosted a luncheon for the marchers and arranged for them to meet with local Mexican-American leaders. Altogether, Fresno was a delightful experience for everyone. The marchers left with renewed spirit and enthusiasm for their task.

On the fourteenth day of the march, Chavez did something that his brother Manuel, Jim Drake, and just about everybody else in NFWA did not want him to do: He talked with Bill Kircher, national director of organizing for AFL-CIO. Kircher was Big Labor, Chavez's friends said. They could prove that he couldn't be trusted with one item in the local newspaper, headlined "AFL-CIO Boycotts March." The article quoted the opinion of "an AFL-CIO spokesman" that the campesinos' march was a civil rights demonstration having no relation at all to unionism.

Chavez met with Kircher anyway and called the surprising statement to his attention. Kircher was furious. "I'll be back,"

# The Corrido of Cesar Chavez

*The pilgrimage to Sacramento gave La Causa another corrido, which Stan Steiner translated for* La Raza: The Mexican Americans.

The seventeenth of March
First Thursday morning of Lent,
Cesar walked from Delano,
Taking with him his faith.

When we arrive in Fresno,
All the people shout:
Long live Cesar Chavez,
And all who follow him.

Now we reach Stockton.
The mariachis sing to us:
Long live Cesar Chavez,
And the Virgin who guides him.

*Enduring fatigue and the pain of severely blistered feet, Chavez leads marchers to Sacramento.*

Listen Señor Cesar Chavez,
Your name is honored;
On your breast you wear
The Virgin of Guadalupe.

United Auto Workers president Walter Reuther (center, front), who marched during the December 1965 strike along with other union members to show the AFL-CIO's support for La Causa, also supported Chavez's march to Sacramento.

he said; then he got in his car and drove away. The next evening, Chavez found out what the Big Labor organizer had done. When the campesinos marched into Modesto, both sides of the street were lined with representatives from every AFL-CIO union in town. "They were standing there holding signs," Kircher remembered. "'Asbestos Workers Local 1215, Viva La Huelga!' 'Glaziers Union Local 79, Viva La Causa!' Bricklayers, carpenters, painters, all of them."[48]

It was hardly a spontaneous display, but it was welcome nonetheless. Two days later the marchers arrived in Stockton, where cheering supporters pelted them with flowers and mariachi bands filled the cool night air with music. That evening, while Chavez was getting ready for the usual rally, he got a phone call from a man who said he represented Schenley Wines. The company was ready to deal.

Temporarily leaving the peregrinación, Chavez rushed to the home of

*On Easter morning, 1966, the NFWA marchers reached Sacramento and were greeted by a crowd of ten thousand supporters. Here Chavez announced that he had reached an agreement with Schenley Wines. The workers would receive the nation's first farm labor contract.*

Schenley executive Sidney Korshak in Beverly Hills. Bill Kircher was there with some other AFL-CIO people, and so were the Teamsters. The animosity between the AFL-CIO and the Teamsters, who had been expelled from the parent labor organization nearly a decade before, made Korshak's house seem like a war zone with wall-to-wall carpet and custom drapes.

Kircher refused to deal with Teamsters and the Teamsters were none too happy about dealing with him. Korshak just wanted to deal with somebody who could speak for the farm workers and put an end to the boycott. After all was said and done, that "somebody" turned out to be Cesar Chavez. Together, the man from Delano and the man from Beverly Hills hammered out a contract. Then Chavez rushed to Sacramento in time to join the march as it reached the state capitol building on Easter Sunday morning, April 11, 1966.

Ten thousand well-wishers joined the celebration in drizzling rain. It was there that Chavez announced the contract with Schenley Wines. Aside from pineapple workers in Hawaii, who were covered by the International Longshoremen's and Warehousemen's Union, the Schenley agreement was the first farm labor contract in the history of American agriculture. Chavez was determined that it would not be the last.

# 8 Matters of Survival

Success breeds success, or so the adage goes, and nobody knew this better than Cesar Chavez. Other California wineries followed Schenley's lead: Almaden, Gallo, Christian Brothers, Paul Masson, all signed contracts with the union. On the heels of these first victories, Chavez turned the boycott against a new target: DiGiorgio Foods, world's largest shipper of fresh fruit.

DiGiorgio was a giant of American agribusiness, Goliath to NFWA's David. With a reputation for harshness in dealing with unions, DiGiorgio had won every skirmish with labor for nearly forty years and had grown to enormous proportions. The company owned nearly five thousand acres of vineyards near Delano and twelve to fifteen thousand acres in other parts of California. They also had thousands of acres in fruit trees, and owned both S&W Fine Foods and TreeSweet Products.

## Unholy Alliances

Though sheer size made DiGiorgio a formidable opponent, it also made it a vulnerable target for the boycott. No company was more visible, with national brand names that consumers could recog-

nize—and avoid. As Chavez told Jacques Levy:

> The boycott . . . began to pick up speed right away. There were a lot of people who had fought DiGiorgio in the thirties and the forties and the fifties who started coming out of the

*Chavez's success in negotiating labor contracts with the wine industry gave him the momentum to take on the world's largest shipper of fresh fruit, DiGiorgio Foods.*

woodwork to take them on in Chicago, San Francisco, New York. We had the most effective boycott in the shortest period of time of any of our boycotts.[49]

When DiGiorgio asked to begin negotiations in May 1966, Chavez dared to hope that NFWA was getting somewhere. It turned out that he was wrong. While he was negotiating with DiGiorgio executives in Fresno, armed guards were threatening picketers in Delano, and company officials were firing anybody with a record of union activity.

Chavez promptly broke off the talks until DiGiorgio disarmed the company's guards and stopped their harassment of NFWA members. DiGiorgio appeared to yield gracefully to these demands but remained hard at work behind the scenes. Before long, Chavez began to hear disturbing rumors of Teamster organizers coming into the fields, trying to get people to join their union. When the Teamster contingent had appeared at the Schenley negotiations, Chavez had not understood why they'd come. Now he realized the danger his union faced.

The International Brotherhood of Teamsters, Chauffeurs, Warehousemen, and Helpers of America was the biggest and wealthiest union in the country. According to government and law enforce-

## The Virtue of Loyalty

*In his book* Latinos: A Biography of the People, *Earl Shorris discusses the cultural base of the loyalty that bound the farm workers to Cesar Chavez.*

"This sense of loyalty grows out of a connection to land, family, and church. It is strongest in Puerto Ricans, Mexicans, and Central Americans, all of whom have ties to their home towns or districts. . . . The sense of loyalty to place devolves from the earlier rural life in which place and family were synonymous. . . . Latinos learn their place in a larger hierarchy from the Catholic Church, which gives lessons in loyalty and obedience, and imparts to all its followers the sense of a structured world in which each person plays an unquestioning role. . . . Even before the Church, family ties teach enduring lessons of loyalty, creating the structure that the other aspects reinforce by repetition. The Latino world builds outward from the life-giving center of home, church, and town. The person belongs to the group, relies on the group, is a person by virtue of belonging. A Latino carries his mother's as well as his father's name. A whole person has parents, family, and is so defined."

*The Teamsters, America's largest union, was also one of the most corrupt. DiGiorgio Foods turned to the Teamsters to intimidate picketers and guard fields.*

ment agencies, it was also the most corrupt. Accused of racketeering and connections with organized crime, the union had been kicked out of the AFL-CIO in 1957. Teamster president Dave Beck went to prison for his part in illegal activities; his replacement, James R. "Jimmy" Hoffa, was under investigation by the Justice Department.

When NFWA became a problem, DiGiorgio had turned to the Teamsters, with their reputation for cutthroat tactics and "sweetheart" contracts (agreements that favored employers at the expense of the workers). While the Teamsters organized in the fields, NFWA picketed outside the fences. But on May 20, 1966, DiGiorgio obtained a court order severely limiting the number of pickets the strikers could use.

For Chavez's people, this was a terrible blow; picketing was the best weapon they had. It dramatized the workers' message to the public and also put pressure on strikebreakers in the fields. Some of the NFWA members were so frustrated that they began to wonder whether the time for peaceful measures had passed; they seemed to be running out of nonviolent ideas.

## The Art of Peaceful Militancy

With his abiding faith in the people, Chavez called a meeting to ask NFWA members for their help: "A couple of hours later," he told Jacques Levy, "three ladies said they wanted to see me. . . . First they wanted to make sure that I wouldn't be offended by what they wanted to tell me. Then they wanted to assure me that they were not trying to tell me how to run the strike." Their next question was about the injunction against picketing. They listened carefully to Chavez's answer. "What would happen," one of them asked, "if we met across the street from the DiGiorgio gates, not to picket, not to demonstrate, but to have a prayer, maybe a mass?"[50]

That was all it took to set Cesar's mind spinning. He and Richard found a picture of Our Lady of Guadalupe and set up a shrine in the back of an old station wagon,

### A Matter of Image

*Chavez's methods did not appeal to all farm workers, as Frank Bardacke noted in a newspaper article about the UFW.*

"The manipulative use of farm workers gave the union boycott its texture and feel. In the mid-'70s, a story circulated in Salinas about a union meeting in the Imperial Valley called to recruit workers to go to a press conference in Los Angeles to support one of the boycotts. For the workers it meant a 10-hour round-trip on one of their days off, but many of them were willing to do it. These particular farm workers were mostly young piece-rate lettuce cutters who earned relatively high wages, and who, like a lot of working-class people able to afford it, put their money into clothes and cars which they sported on their days off. They were a proud people, volunteering to spend a weekend in Los Angeles organizing support for their movement. As the meeting closed, Marshall Ganz . . . had a final request. At the press conference everybody should wear their work clothes. The union officials didn't want farm workers to appear as regular working people appealing for solidarity. They had to be poor and suffering, hats in hand, asking for charity. It may have made a good press conference, but the people who told the story were angered and shamed."

complete with candles and flowers. Somehow it seemed right: a movable shrine for a movable people. The next morning, the car was parked across from the DiGiorgio gates, and the campesinos' mass began. That first day, hundreds came to worship at the humble little outdoor chapel. The nonstop prayer meeting lasted for two months. Chavez considered it a heartwarming testament to the quiet power of nonviolence, but he also knew that one symbolic victory would not win the struggle.

DiGiorgio was skilled at breaking strikes, and the Teamsters knew how to squeeze rivals out of the picture. What could a small and poorly financed union do against such powerful adversaries? The question nagged Chavez in the daytime and haunted his dreams at night. He had always insisted on NFWA independence from Big Labor as well as Big Business and Big Government. When he thought of the long and costly struggle that lay ahead, he had to admit that NFWA needed allies. He turned to Bill Kircher of the AFL-CIO.

## Free and Open Elections

By summer of 1966, NFWA seemed to be making progress with DiGiorgio. Their organizers were still barred from entering Di-Giorgio's fields to talk with the workers, but the company had agreed to allow elections. Chavez and Bill Kircher went to San Francisco to meet with company attorney Donald Connors. They were hammering out rules for an election that would let Di-Giorgio workers decide who, if anyone, should represent them in negotiations with the company. The choice would be between NFWA, Teamsters, and "no union."

Chavez felt confident that NFWA could win an honest election. He was in good spirits when he and Kircher left that first meeting. They had settled a few issues and agreed to meet again in two days' time to continue negotiations. That same night, they learned that DiGiorgio had already set up its own elections, complete with polling places, printed ballots, and a press conference to explain that the company meant to "do right" by its workers.

Bill Kircher was outraged. Fuming, he announced his intention to break up Di-Giorgio's press conference with a good dose of truth. Chavez organized a boycott of the election and Kircher tried to stop it through the courts, but nothing they did made any difference. Unfair though it was, the election went ahead. Unsurprisingly, the Teamsters won, leaving Chavez and his people to lick their wounds and cry foul.

DiGiorgio's rigged election, which occurred on June 24, 1966, shaped the remainder of the summer. To Chavez and his tired, often disheartened workers, only one thing mattered: getting that election declared invalid and setting up a new one. This time the struggle turned ugly and the police were unable, or unwilling, to do anything about it. Teamsters followed NFWA members around town and harassed them on the picket lines, swaggering, boasting, and threatening at every turn. When they beat up four NFWA pickets, Chavez knew he had to act before Delano exploded with the violence he had tried so desperately to avoid. He turned to Kircher, who made a couple of phone calls.

A few hours later, fourteen burly members of the Seafarers Union showed up in Delano. Their orders were simple: Let the Teamsters know you are around, but travel

*Chavez walks through a crowd of supporters who carry the NFWA eagle alongside a crucifix. The spiritual dimension of the movement motivated many strikers to persevere, though not everyone agreed with the approach.*

in pairs, and use no violence. With the Seafarers on hand, the beatings and harassment stopped. Chavez loved it; nonviolent though he was, he could still enjoy watching a Seafarer, with arms bigger than most people's legs, back down an attacker with a single, withering look. As the summer wore on, there was uneasy peace in the streets of Delano.

## A New Election

Chavez and Kircher convinced the governor, Edmund G. "Pat" Brown, to appoint an independent investigator to study the election of June 24. Brown chose Dr. Ronald Haughton of the American Arbitration Association, who weighed the facts and recommended a new election, to be supervised by the Arbitration Association.

Getting the rigged June 24 election set aside was a big victory for NFWA. Chavez knew it never would have happened without help from Kircher and the AFL-CIO. For the first time in his career as an organizer, he began to think that joining with the "big boys" might not be such a bad idea after all. He talked to Dolores Huerta, Marshall Ganz, Jim Drake, and several other members of his inner circle about merging with AWOC to form a new AFL-CIO affiliate. Then he went straight to Kircher. He knew that some people would question this move, but he also knew that affiliation was the best way for the union to survive—perhaps the only way. Speaking of the decision later, Chavez told Peter Matthiessen:

We were an independent union at the beginning. We were not part of the AFL, or anybody else, because we didn't want interference in the way we thought things had to be done. Too many mistakes can be made by unions trying to organize workers, and too much money would be an obstacle, at least in the beginning, because people who give it can tell you what to do with it. . . . Money for money's sake is nothing.[51]

## Joining Forces

Most of the farm workers went along with the merger; it was the student volunteers who opposed it. These young veterans of the civil rights, free speech, and anti-Viet Nam War movements had been tireless in working for La Causa. Now they felt betrayed: Cesar Chavez, their stubborn, clever, courageous leader had sold out to Big Labor. After the merger, many of these volunteers lost interest and drifted away; others covered their retreat with a storm of bitter accusations against Big Government, Big Labor, and Cesar Chavez.

Through the endless debates that surrounded the merger, the Mexican-American farm workers never wavered in their devotion to Chavez. Many of the Anglo volunteers and the AFL organizers were puzzled by this unquestioning loyalty, but Jim Drake had been around Mexican culture long enough to understand *aguantar*, even though he didn't use the word in describing the concept to Peter Matthiessen:

Mexico is a poor land . . . the natural suffering [due to poverty] has been rit-

ualized, institutionalized, especially in the work of the Franciscans. Mexicans didn't respond much to the missionaries who came with the conquistadors, but when Junipero Serra, the first Franciscan, landed at Acapulco and walked barefoot to Mexico City, this was something they could understand. Mexicans believe that from suffering you get strength rather than death. This is expressed in penitential acts and especially in the Eucharist [the Catholic mass]. . . . Of the strike, people are saying, "We've always suffered. Now we can suffer for a purpose."[52]

The new union took a new name: the United Farm Workers Organizing Committee (UFWOC). Chavez's first official act was to get ready for the upcoming election. His second was to march into the Stockton office and whip Al Green's operation into shape. Though a capable administrator, Green, who had retired at the time of the merger, was an "old style" labor organizer. His staff people were used to earning $125 per week, which was a respectable salary at that time, and they were not willing to make the sacrifices that Chavez demanded. All of them quit, except for Larry Itliong who remained as sturdy and faithful as ever.

On August 30, 1966, under supervision of the American Arbitration Association, the workers at DiGiorgio's Sierra Vista ranch in Delano turned out by the hundreds to exercise their right to the ballot. UFWOC won. Some weeks later, the union won a similar election at DiGiorgio's Arvin ranch. When reports of the victories hit newspapers and television, Chavez received a congratulatory telegram he would never forget:

As brothers in the fight for equality, I extend the hand of fellowship and good will and wish continuing success to you and your members. The fight for equality must be fought on many fronts—in the urban slums, in the sweat shops of the factories and fields. Our separate struggles are really one—a struggle for freedom, for dignity, and for humanity. You and your valiant fellow workers have demonstrated your commitment to righting grievous wrongs forced upon exploited people. We are together with you in spirit and in determination that our dreams for a better tomorrow will be realized.[53]

It was signed "Martin Luther King Jr."

## The Next Crusade

Inspired by their success, the UFWOC staff wanted to target Giumarra, largest grower of table grapes in the region.

*The UFWOC's strike against Giumarra, the largest grower of table grapes in the Delano region, spread quickly across the United States. Here, picketers in New York City join the national movement to open negotiations between growers and workers.*

## What Do the Farm Workers Want?

*The farm workers' agenda became part of the* Congressional Record *for October 11, 1968. In* Sal Si Puedes, *Peter Matthiessen includes a passage from the* Congressional Record *summarizing the goals that Chavez and UFWOC had affirmed.*

"The primary goal is to obtain union recognition and assurance of good faith collective bargaining from their grower and farmer employers.

The best way to achieve this goal would be to include the agricultural industry under the protective provisions of the National Labor Relations Act [so that farm workers] can work together with their employers toward: A living wage, so that their children do not have to quit grammar school to help earn food;

Sanitary facilities placed in the fields to protect themselves, and the consumer, from disease;

The right to work and live with dignity . . . ;

. . . Collective bargaining agreements . . . that provide for higher wages, grievance procedures, overtime pay, job security, rest periods, health insurance, holidays and vacations with pay, and other benefits."

---

Chavez was not sure. "I wasn't too hot on going just after Giumarra," he told Jacques Levy. "I was afraid we'd establish a pattern of going after growers one at a time, and if the domino theory didn't work, it would take us thirty years to get all the Delano growers.[54]

Though Chavez eventually gave in to the enthusiasm of the staff, it soon became obvious that a strike would not be enough. Giumarra obtained a court injunction that allowed only two pickets at each entrance to the ranch. With too many nonunion workers in the fields and too few strikers on the picket lines, the labor action sputtered until Chavez decided to fall back on the one technique that had served him well in the past: boycott. His strategy this time was bold and direct. Forty farm workers and ten student volunteers set off for New York City in the union's rickety yellow bus. None of them had ever organized a boycott before, but they were about to get a crash course in activism with the nation's largest city as their classroom. After that, they would spearhead a coordinated national movement that would shut down the market for table grapes and open up meaningful negotiations between growers and workers.

# 9 Times of Sacrifice and Sorrow

When the boycott showed signs of taking hold, Giumarra began to ship grapes under different labels. Chavez spelled out the ploy for Jacques Levy:

> First they had six, then in less than sixty days they had about sixty. Soon we were dealing with over a hundred. Although it was against the law, they were using the labels of all the California growers against us. . . . Our own troops were confused. They didn't know which labels to boycott, which not to boycott. People who wanted to help also were confused.[55]

Fred Ross and Dolores Huerta had a simple countermeasure to this tactic: boycott all California table grapes. Chavez did not like the idea of a general boycott, but he soon realized that it might be the only weapon the union had left. With a clear target, organizers would be more effective and consumers more willing to go along. That, at least, was the theory; Chavez could only hope and pray that it would work.

## A Sacrificial Offering

Even with the expanded boycott, results were slow in coming. By February 1968,

the strikers were running out of patience; a mood of frustration and even rebellion swept through the ranks. Activities that had been peaceful took a disturbing turn toward violence. Arsonists set fire to several packing sheds, and Chavez found guns on the picket line. He knew then that it was time for another graphic lesson in the principles of nonviolence.

On Thursday, February 15, 1968, Chavez stopped eating. The following Monday he called a union meeting to announce what he was doing. He would continue the fast, he said, until every UFWOC member had renewed his or her commitment to nonviolence. Then he turned and walked out of the hall. People sat in stunned silence; some of them afraid, some annoyed. Then they began to argue.

It was no accident that the fast had begun during the season of Lent, the weeks of penitence and self-denial when Christians prepare for Easter. Chavez even gave up the comforts of home and family, choosing to spend the fast in an unheated adobe building across from the Delano City Dump. The "co-op," as it was called, stood on a forty-acre parcel UFWOC had bought from a member who could no longer afford the property taxes. Someday it would be a great complex, housing shops, a gas station, and a medical clinic

*The barren adobe building where Chavez spent twenty-five days fasting in an unheated, windowless storeroom. Chavez chose to fast here to draw attention to the UFWOC's grape boycott and to demonstrate his commitment to nonviolence.*

as well as the meeting hall. For the moment it was empty and strangely silent, with nothing but the cool, earthy reality of adobe and red clay tile. It reminded Chavez of the farmhouse of his childhood, with its breezeways and whitewashed walls.

He chose a windowless storeroom for his quarters and there the drama of his sacrificial offering unfolded: "It was tragic and portentous," wrote Stan Steiner. "[Cesar] offered his body in a 'Lenten Fast for Peace and Nonviolence' that lasted for twenty-five days. He sacrificed one-fifth of his flesh, thirty-five pounds, to 'the pain and suffering of the farm workers.'"[56]

Many of the UFWOC's most dedicated volunteers were puzzled by the fast. What good could it possibly do? They simply did not understand. It was too "Mexican" for the Anglos to figure out, and too "Catholic" for the agnostics, Protestants, and Jews. Protestant Epifiano Camacho saw no reason for such a self-destructive

act. Tony Orendain, a former Catholic, was furious. For him, the fast was not only an embarrassment, it was an affront to the very people Chavez wanted to help. *Los pobres* (the poor) had long suffered from the notion that poverty was somehow their fault—and that penitence could perhaps make them "worthy" of a better life.

Even Helen, who was Catholic, Mexican, and accustomed to her husband's notions of self-sacrifice, pronounced the fast "ridiculous." While he fasted at Forty Acres, she was home taking care of eight children and worrying that her husband would do permanent damage to his health. Only later, when the fast was over and the danger past, did Cesar realize how frightened Helen had been.

A few of his colleagues did understand, if not with their minds, then with their hearts: "I know it's hard for people who are not Mexican," said Dolores Huerta, ". . . but this is part of the Mexican

## Stating the Case

*On May 10, 1969, to let the table grape growers know they meant business, the union issued its Boycott Day Proclamation. The passage quoted here is from* A Documentary History of the Mexican Americans, *edited by Wayne Moquin and Charles Van Doren.*

"We the striking grape workers of California, join on the International Boycott Day with the consumers across the continent in planning the steps that lie ahead on the road to our liberation. As we plan, we recall the events that brought us to this day and the events of this day. . . . We have been farm workers for hundreds of years and pioneers for seven. Mexicans, Filipinos, Africans and others, our ancestors were among those who founded this land and tamed its natural wilderness and we are pioneers who blaze a trail out of the wilderness and of hunger and deprivation. . . . We have been farm workers for hundreds of years and strikers for four. . . . We mean to have our peace, and to win it without violence. . . . We have been farm workers for hundreds of years and boycotters for two. . . . We marched alone at the beginning but today we count men of all creeds, nationalities, and occupations in our number. . . . They pledge to withhold their patronage from stores that handle grapes during the boycott, just as we withhold our labor from the growers until our dispute is resolved."

culture—the penance, the whole idea of suffering for something, of self-inflicted punishment."[57] To Chavez, fasting was more than a symbolic gesture. It had real power. Picketing and boycotting could only draw attention to a problem—fasting could solve it.

## A Time of Renewal

Chavez's fast became the center of a Lenten pilgrimage as people came to Forty Acres to renew their commitment to nonviolence and the principles of La Causa. In twenty-five days, this determined act of penance not only reshaped the union, but affected people all over the nation. Both Martin Luther King Jr. and Robert Kennedy sent telegrams to express their sympathy and support. Chavez's old friend Walter Reuther donated $50,000 to build a meeting hall at Forty Acres.

As the drama unfolded, there was even an occasional bit of comic relief. Chavez loved to tell the story of "the taco man," a stranger who slipped into his room with a bag of tacos and ordered him to eat. When Chavez refused, the man got desperate. He had come all the way from Merced, he confided; people back there were counting on him. They had sent him to Delano to break the fast before the fast broke Chavez, and this he was determined to do. When Chavez would not agree to eat, the stranger lunged at him. The two men struggled until the would-be Good Samaritan was on top of Chavez, with one hand pinning him to the bed and the other trying to force food into his mouth.

Richard came in and saw someone apparently trying to throttle his brother. When he yelled for help, half a dozen people shoved into the room and wrestled the stranger to the floor. Over the scuffling and the yelling, Cesar shouted for them to stop. The stranger meant no harm, he said, and explained what had happened. After apologies all around, the man from Merced left with nothing worse than rumpled clothing and a bag full of squashed tacos.

When Chavez was ready to break the fast he did it as publicly as possible, wringing every last bit of ceremony from the moment. On the appointed day, March 10, 1968, about eight thousand people attended a mass at Forty Acres; among them was Senator Robert Kennedy, who chartered a plane to be present for the ceremony. It was this wealthy and powerful son

*Surrounded by a crowd of nearly eight thousand people, Robert Kennedy breaks bread with Chavez, ending the labor organizer's month-long hunger strike.*

of a legendary family who gave Chavez the bread that ended his ordeal. They sat together through a religious celebration that opened with a prayer by a Jewish rabbi, continued with a sermon delivered by a Protestant minister, and ended with a mass performed by a Roman Catholic priest.

At Forty Acres that day, no ordinary service could have captured the feelings of people of all races, creeds, and economic classes who had come together for a common purpose. It was there that farm workers begged Senator Kennedy to run for president; six days later, he formally declared himself a candidate. To the end of his days, Chavez believed that the mass at Forty Acres had helped persuade the senator to run.

To commemorate Cesar's sacrifice, Richard Chavez fashioned a thirty-foot cross out of telephone poles. A crew of volunteers raised it at the place where Cesar broke the fast and someone planted climbing vines at its base. People would place offerings of fresh flowers on the cross, much as they might adorn an altar or a gravestone. Twice vandals tried to burn Cesar's cross and twice they failed. Then one morning, the people of Forty Acres found it lying in the dust, cut down by someone with a power saw and a grudge.

## All My Sorrows

Less than three months after Chavez's fast, both Martin Luther King Jr. and Robert Kennedy were dead, shot down by assassins. Chavez was stunned by the deaths of the minister who had been his role model and the senator who had been his friend. Beyond his personal grief was a political question. Who would the farm workers support in the upcoming presidential election now that Kennedy was gone?

In the long hot summer of 1968, the Democrats went to Chicago for a slugfest that masqueraded as a political convention. Out of the bitterness and rancor of that gathering, Lyndon Johnson's vice president, Hubert Humphrey, became the Democratic nominee. The Republicans chose Richard Nixon, who had served as vice president under Dwight D. Eisenhower. Chavez could not support either candidate; for him, the election that might have been a boon to farm workers came down to a choice between the lesser of two evils.

Not long after Kennedy's death, Chavez faced another challenge, this one deeply personal and beyond his ability to control. Through all the hardships of his life, he had remained in excellent physical health. Then came a day he would never forget:

> I arrived home from a UAW Labor Day picnic, walked in the door, and turned to close it when I had a severe pain like a knife through my back. I couldn't move, I wanted to die. For a good twenty minutes I stood frozen. Finally I was given some aspirin and was able to go to bed.[58]

That was the beginning of months of pain and disability. Nothing the doctors could do—in the hospital or out—seemed to help. The condition occurred because one of Chavez's legs was shorter than the other. Years of compensating for the difference had finally caused painful spasms that made it impossible for him to stand.

Chavez conducted UFWOC business from his sickbed, but still his condition took a toll on morale. People had grown accustomed to his hands-on style of leadership; without it there was a void.

## New Battles to Fight

In the midst of the crisis presented by Chavez's illness, DiGiorgio finalized the sale of its agricultural properties in Delano and Arvin. This was another setback for the union because there was no "successor clause" in UFWOC's contracts. Thus the new owners were not bound by DiGiorgio's agreements. One of Chavez's shining accomplishments crumbled before his eyes, and he was powerless to stop it. Under any circumstances that would have been de-pressing; in combination with his failing health it was very nearly devastating.

Just when Chavez felt unable to take any more adversity, a man known only as "Monares" revealed a plot against his life. Monares said that he had been present when a group of labor contractors discussed hiring a "shooter" to assassinate Chavez. This was not the first death threat, but it was the first one that sounded like a genuine danger. With the King and Kennedy assassinations still painfully fresh in everyone's mind, the union tightened security around its bedridden leader. Guards stayed with him around the clock, and so did a German shepherd named Boycott. Chavez had never owned a dog, but Boycott became a valued companion as well as a protective bodyguard.

Living daily with pain and the threat of violent death, Chavez took refuge in his

### Return of the *Coyotes*

*In the* Los Angeles Times *of October 17, 1993, reporter Fred Alvarez described the renewed influence of labor contractors in the agricultural workplace.*

"The hunt for work begins while the barrio is still dark. Drawn by the hope of a day's pay, farm workers collect in a poor pocket of Oxnard hours before first light bleeds into the sky—a scene played out daily at hiring sites throughout the state. . . . Hundreds of laborers have joined the hunt by the time the labor contractors arrive.

In their dented pickups and old vans, the contractors are the mightiest men in the barrio for the moment. . . . California's $18-billion farm industry has become dominated by independent contractors. No one is sure how many there are, but more than 1,000 are licensed statewide and many more wield power without official blessing."

*Chavez with his German shepherds Boycott and Huelga. Boycott acted as a protective bodyguard and a loyal friend after Chavez received a serious death threat.*

work. There was certainly enough of it to keep him busy. By 1969, the union had forged the boycott into a devastating weapon and was expanding into health and safety issues. Chavez assigned a former high school principal and a nurse to shape the union's health care programs. In the progress of their work, Leroy Chatfield and Marion Moses came face to face with the threat of agricultural chemicals.

Most of the workers who came to a union-run clinic for treatment suffered from complaints that were directly or indirectly related to poverty and lack of sanitary facilities. But a substantial number of the more serious illnesses were caused by exposure to hazardous pesticides. The union had been dealing with pesticide issues for some time, but these clinical findings brought the dangers into new focus. In targeting the indiscriminate use of agricultural chemicals, Cesar Chavez fired one of the earliest salvos in what was to become the environmental movement.

# Tightening the Noose

On May 10, 1969, a carefully worded proclamation ushered in a new thrust in the long-running boycott of California table grapes. City by city, Chavez and his volunteers closed down the market for grapes until tons of them rotted in cold storage and the growers were on the edge of capitulation. It was like a war now, or maybe a chess game, each side developing its strategies and maneuvering for position. Despite his gentle nature, Chavez was good at this game; after all, he had been practicing for most of his life. He had also been practicing the poor man's virtue, which is patience. *Hay más tiempo que vida,* he often said, which meant that time was on his side.

Not until the summer of 1970 was there finally a breakthrough. The boycott was tight and the growers were hurting when Chavez got word that Philip Feick of the Western Employers Council wanted to negotiate. Feick had authorization not only from Giumarra but from twenty-two other companies. Chavez could scarcely believe that a solution was at hand. Excited now, and hopeful, he called an immediate meeting for the afternoon of July 16, but he would not tell anyone the purpose of that meeting.

When people arrived they found the hall set up for mass and a priest standing ready to conduct the service. Chavez hardly said a word to anyone, but there was a sense of controlled excitement in his manner. When the mass was finished, he stood up and said he had a few announcements: There is a strike in Ventura County, another in Colorado—and oh, by the way, twenty-three companies had asked to open negotiations with UFWOC. The cheer was deafening, growing louder and more enthusiastic as Chavez carefully read off each and every one of the names.

Less than two weeks later, the negotiations came to a triumphant close. The original twenty-three growers plus six who had come aboard later agreed to all the provisions Chavez considered most important: a hiring hall, protection against pesticides, $1.80 an hour, with a raise to $2.05 in 1972, plus regular employer contributions to the Health and Welfare and Economic Development funds. After five long years, the grape strike was almost over!

The formal signing of agreements took place at Forty Acres. Chavez made sure the ceremony was rich with unforgettable images: flags and speeches and handshakes all around. Even the location was symbolic; the ceremony took place in Reuther Hall, the auditorium that Chavez had named for the friend whose donation made the development possible.

Richard Chavez described that historic gathering for Jacques Levy:

> The growers came in through the back door because the hall was full of people. The only empty seats were at the head table where there were microphones. So they filed in one by one, someone from each company, and sat down facing the people. [John Giumarra Jr., son of the company president,] made a speech that finally peace had come to the valley, that we were going to work together. It was a great thing. People were very happy, singing and cheering. There were more people outside that couldn't get in. There were twenty-nine contracts signed that day.[59]

*Chavez and John Giumarra Sr. sign labor contracts in 1970, bringing the five-year grape strike to an end. The contracts guaranteed that farm workers would receive wage increases, health benefits, and protection against pesticides.*

## When the Cheering Stopped

Administering the contracts turned out to be almost as difficult as winning them in the first place. Immediately after the signing, Cesar was called out of town on urgent business. He left Richard to administer the new Delano contracts.

By Richard's own admission, that early organizing was a disaster. He had to get in-

formation from hundreds of workers, sign people up for union benefit programs, and develop an efficient procedure for dispatching workers from the hiring hall. His only help was a group of young, inexperienced volunteers from Los Angeles. Nobody seemed to know what anybody else was doing. Information cards got lost, misfiled, or duplicated; some members were charged twice for the same month's dues, while others did not get charged at all. The hiring hall was bedlam, with a skeleton crew of volunteers trying to match workers with that day's job orders.

The situation got so bad that one disgusted volunteer sent Cesar a twenty-page report detailing the problems. That brought matters to a head, as Richard told Jacques Levy:

> So Cesar called me. I've got all of this pressure about to the cracking point. . . . I had just finished that day, it was about 11:00 at night, and he just didn't even wait for me to explain anything. He just got on me. . . . I finally hung up on him.[60]

The brothers patched up their differences the next day, but the argument made Cesar realize how much La Causa was changing. The flair for strategy and symbol that had worked so well in the initial struggle might be less effective in a world of rules, regulations, and forms filled out in triplicate. He promised himself that he would not allow UFWOC to become just another bureaucracy, set in its ways and unresponsive to the needs of its members.

"Our goals have to be broader than the traditional goals of unions," he once told an interviewer. "It is more than a union as we know it today that we have to build. It is a movement. It is a movement of the poor. . . . [We] have organized a cooperative movement . . . a community of the poor."[61] It was this dream that kept Chavez going as La Causa faced a new era in its development.

# 10 A Living Legend

Through the seventies and into the eighties, Chavez continued the struggle. There were more strikes, more marches, and more fasts. In 1972 the union received its permanent charter from the AFL-CIO, dropping "Organizing Committee" from its name to become simply the "United Farm Workers of America" (UFW). Three years later, Chavez helped Governor Jerry Brown of California enact the nation's first farm labor law, extending unemployment benefits to farm workers and recognizing their right to organize and bargain collectively. In September 1984 he launched a worldwide boycott of grapes to protest the use of cancer-causing pesticides.

Along the way, Cesar Chavez became a folk hero. Of all the "Cesar stories" that have circulated through the barrios and labor camps of California, the most persistent is *the Bribe*, in which a mysterious ever-present "they" offer Chavez a million dollars to betray the farm workers, and he not only turns them down but tells them off.

## A Man of Flesh and Blood

Like most such tales, the Bribe has some basis in fact. Perhaps Chavez never turned

*Helen and Cesar Chavez pose with six of their eight children. Though Cesar's dedication to his work left him little time to spend with his family, Helen remained a source of constant support.*

## Chavez's Control of Union Business

*After the UFW settled down to the business of day-to-day functioning, Chavez's hands-on style of management annoyed some people. Former UFW worker Aristeo Zambrano explained his view of the problem to journalist Frank Bardacke:*

"In the mid-70's, when I became an activist, Chavez was making every decision in the union. If a car in Salinas needed a new tire, we had to check with Cesar in La Paz. He controlled every detail of union business. . . . I remember in particular a closed meeting, just before the Salinas [UFW] convention in 1979. He called together about 20 of us . . . and told us he was going to call off the [Salinas lettuce] strike and send us on the boycott. We refused, and we told him so . . . [and] that meeting, and its aftermath, was a political challenge to Cesar. It meant that the situation in the union had changed. He was going to have to deal with us . . . and, in some way or other, share power with us. And that was what he could not do. He was incapable of sharing power."

down a fortune, but he did turn down jobs with status, security, and a decent salary. His poverty was by choice rather than necessity. In 1969 writer Stan Steiner offered this explanation:

He enacts his beliefs in his body. His family lives in conspicuous poverty. A wife and eight children share a small, two-bedroom frame house in the barrio of Delano. In the era of affluent unionism, such a way of life is an anomaly for a union leader. But it is not martyrdom. The humility of his material goods is an aspect of his philosophy. He believes, as Gandhi did, that the leader of the poor has to live as the poor do, not for their sake, but for his own; the sanctity of his soul and peace of mind demand it of him. . . . Sacrifice is a principle. The poor can-

not afford to suffer it so the leader must suffer it for them.[62]

Chavez's dedication to his chosen work bordered on the fanatical. Though he often neglected his family to handle union business, he never questioned the necessity of that choice or his right to make it. He expected Helen to understand, and fortunately she did. Though she was an intensely private person, she encouraged Cesar in his work and was always there to be a sounding board for his ideas. The children were not so accommodating. Try as he would, Cesar could not persuade them to dedicate their lives to the deep purpose that motivated his own. At one point eldest son Fernando learned to play golf, an unthinkably frivolous pursuit by the standards of his father, who told Peter Matthiessen:

They think I'm pretty old fashioned. I make a lot of fun of people who give their spare time to mowing the lawn, washing their cars, or playing golf. To me it's such a waste of time. How can you justify doing that sort of thing as long as these other things are going on, the suffering?[63]

Chavez expected absolute loyalty and total dedication from everyone around him. Staff members were supposed to be available to the union at any time of the day or night; those who insisted on a personal life outside La Causa did not last for long. It is a tribute to Chavez's leadership that so many were willing to make the required commitment.

## A Changing World

Others were not, and in time the gap between Chavez's vision and practical considerations began to widen. Frank Bardacke summarized the union's declining influence in an article in the *Sacramento Bee.*

In the late 70's, at the height of the UFW's strength, some in California agribusiness had come to the conclusion that Chavez's victory was inevitable and that they would have to learn to live with the UFW. Why wasn't the union—with perhaps 50,000 workers under contract and hundreds of militant activists among them—able to seize this historic opportunity?

The short answer is that within the UFW the boycott tail came to wag the farm worker dog. . . . It was an easy mistake to fall into, especially as the failure of the first grape strikes was followed so stunningly by the success of the first grape boycott. The very best farm worker activists, the strongest Chavistas, were removed from the fields and direct contact with farm workers, so they could be sent to work in the boycott offices of major cities . . . from the point of view of spreading the union among the farm workers themselves, [this strategy] was a disaster.[64]

*Chavez speaks to farm workers in 1974. As the union's influence began to decline in the late 1970s, some wondered whether Chavez's leadership style was out of step with the times.*

# The Legacy of Cesar Chavez

*In* Latinos: A Biography of the People, *Earl Shorris placed Chavez's achievements in the broader context of agricultural history:*

"In the 1930s John Steinbeck made heroes of the white Protestants who lost their lands in Oklahoma and Kansas and came through the dust to work the farms of California. He wrote of how they tried to form a union and were beaten down; Woody Guthrie sang of how they tried and were beaten down. Steinbeck's heroes could not organize in the rich, brutal fields. . . . That task waited for Cesar Chavez, a man who knew the dust bowl and the hard life of a farm worker during the Depression. . . . The hunger strike of Cesar Chavez made him an American Gandhi. Nothing Steinbeck wrote, nothing Woody Guthrie sang prepared the world for the unbreakable will, the brown skin, and the beautiful, suffered face of Cesar Chavez."

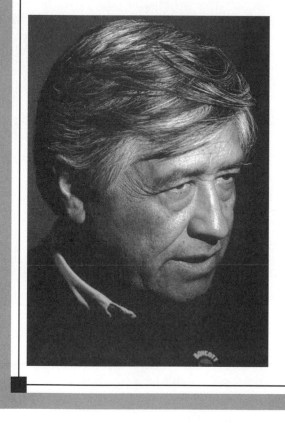

*By dedicating his life to fighting for the rights of farm workers, Cesar Chavez made an important and lasting contribution to American society.*

As troubles mounted and membership plunged, schisms appeared in the union leadership. Some began to say that Chavez was out of step with the times. Tony Orendain became one of the first to break with UFW when he and Chavez fought about organizing farm workers in Texas. Orendain founded the Texas Farm Workers Union, and soon there was a full-scale jurisdictional war that destroyed TFWU and weakened UFW. According to Orendain, this had not been necessary:

We could have stayed in the UFW. People wanted the movement here to continue, but Cesar said there couldn't be two movements. He accused me of being a communist. . . . [T]he worst enemy to us wasn't the ranchers but Cesar Chavez. . . . He thinks that if other groups start up he will lose face and [funding for UFW].[65]

## The Summing Up

Was Cesar Chavez out of step with the times? Perhaps. But that does not change what he accomplished, nor does it reflect his character. Neither the staff members who eventually left UFW nor the growers who despised it ever accused Chavez of being dishonest or insincere. In a tribute published after the UFW leader's death, the *Sacramento Bee* stated: "He was not

---

### The Accomplishments of the Union

*On February 23, 1992, the* Sacramento Bee *featured a partial listing of UFW's achievements since its inception as NFWA in 1962.*

"1966: First collective-bargaining agreement for workers.

1966: First union contract requiring rest periods, clean drinking water, hand-washing facilities, protective clothing against pesticide exposure, and banning pesticide spraying while workers are in the fields.

1967: First union contract restricting the use of dangerous pesticides.

1969: First union health benefits paid for farm workers. . . .

1970: First union contract requiring testing of farm workers . . . to monitor exposure to pesticides.

1970: First union contracts prohibiting job discrimination . . . against women workers.

1975: . . . extension of unemployment benefits to farm workers.

1981: First cost-of-living guarantee in union contract.

1983: Benefits paid under the nation's first and only pension program for retired farm workers. . . .

1987: First profit-sharing program under a union contract. . . .

1991: First union contract providing farm workers with parental leave to care for a sick child, parent, or newborn baby."

*Support for Chavez spread internationally. Here, protesters march with signs as part of the worldwide boycott of grapes.*

merely a labor organizer in the traditional sense, but a spiritual leader who used soft-spoken appeals, self-imposed poverty and frequent fasts to advance his cause."[66]

This spiritual dimension motivated Chavez to persevere in spite of disappointments, reversals, and overwhelming odds. From it came his charismatic power and his talent for weaving rich symbolism into everyday events. Only Cesar Chavez would have carried the banner of the Virgin of Guadalupe into a labor demonstration. Only he would have inspired so many heartfelt corridos, or organized a massive prayer meeting across from a big grower's

gates, or understood the power of that black eagle flag before its spectacular launch.

History is filled with accounts of great warriors who distinguished themselves in battle but could never adjust to the mundane realities of civilian life. Some people believe that this was the case with the non-violent "warrior," Cesar Chavez. Newspaper columnist Dan Walters pointed out the contrast between Chavez's victories as an activist and his difficulties as an administrator:

Chavez could be charismatic enough to attract would-be presidents of the

## Tributes to Cesar Chavez

*The day after Chavez died, people from all over the country eulogized his accomplishments and mourned his loss. Sam Stanton reported some of the tributes in the* Sacramento Bee.

"A lot of us used to almost beg him not to do so many fasts," said Sacramento Mayor Joe Serna Jr., a former organizer for Chavez. "I think those fasts probably took a toll on his health."

"We're still in shock," said Dolores Huerta, vice president emeritus of the UFW and a founding member. "Society lost a very great man. Cesar proved to the world that poor people can solve their problems if they stick together, and he showed the rest of society how they can participate and help the downtrodden."

"Cesar was one of the most charismatic persons that I have ever met in my lifetime," said Loaves & Fishes Director Leroy Chatfield. "And I have met Bobby Kennedy and a lot of nationally ranked people, but he was truly the most charismatic."

United States and show-business notables to his cause, but he could also do things that defied rationality—like pumping hundreds of thousands of dollars into a 1980 squabble among Democrats over the speakership of the [California] state Assembly and thus alienating dozens of politicians who would otherwise have been sympathetic to him and the UFW. . . . He could spend years winning bargaining rights and pay contracts for poor field hands—and then undercut those gains by poorly administering his end of the contracts and allowing his rivals to gain strength.[67]

Even a sketchy listing of his achievements is filled with breakthroughs, from the first collective bargaining agreement in the history of California agriculture to health benefits, pension programs, and even profit sharing. Perhaps Chavez's most important accomplishment was creating a climate of change, in which farm workers could no longer be seen as faceless, disposable "tools" to be obtained as cheaply as possible and used in whatever manner the employer saw fit. The significance of what he did is in no way diminished by what he was not able to do.

Sacramento mayor Joe Serna Jr. called Chavez "the expression of hope for all of us who grew up in farm worker families. He gave us hope when we had lost hope in ourselves and gave us pride not only in being farm workers but in being Mexicans."[68]

Cesar Chavez died in his sleep on April 23, 1993, and his final march was the biggest ever. Twenty-five thousand people of every color and creed marched from

*Actor James Edward Olmos (center) and Joseph Kennedy (behind Olmos) help carry the unadorned pine casket of Cesar Chavez. Twenty-five thousand people joined the three-and-a-half-mile funeral procession in Delano, California, to pay homage to Chavez.*

Delano to Forty Acres, and ten thousand more joined them there. Some of those people were poor, some were rich, some were unknown, and some were famous. None of that mattered. They came to honor a man that all of them had admired.

At the head of the procession were the banners that always led Chavez's marches: the American and Mexican flags, along with the black eagle of the UFW and the standard of the Virgin of Guadalupe. More than a hundred pallbearers took turns carrying the coffin through the streets. It was an unvarnished pine box, made by his brother's hand; a poor man's coffin. No one who saw it could have failed to get the message: "My father," said Fernando Chavez, "chose to live a life of voluntary poverty, and yet I believe his legacy will be rich, a legacy of non-violence, a legacy in the spirit of Gandhi, Martin Luther King and Bobby Kennedy."[69]

Others spoke, sharing memories and grief. Everyone listened and some people cried, and when the service was over they had a fiesta, complete with soda pop and homemade tacos and people singing Mexican songs.

Cesar Chavez would have loved it.

# Notes

### Introduction: The Road Less Traveled

1. Sacramento mayor Joe Serna Jr., quoted in *Sacramento Bee*, April 24, 1993.
2. Sam Stanton, "Farm Workers' Leader Cesar Chavez, 66, Dies," *Sacramento Bee*, April 24, 1993.
3. Quoted in Frank Bardacke, "What Went Wrong with the UFW?" *Sacramento Bee*, August 1, 1993.
4. Quoted in Stanton, "Farm Workers' Leader Cesar Chavez, 66, Dies."
5. Quoted by Peter Hecht and Wayne Wilson, *Sacramento Bee*, April 24, 1993.

### Chapter 1: Hard Times

6. Quoted in Jacques Levy, *Cesar Chavez: Autobiography of La Causa*. New York: Norton, 1975.
7. Quoted in Levy, *Cesar Chavez*.
8. Quoted in Levy, *Cesar Chavez*.

### Chapter 2: The Way of a Man

9. Quoted in Stan Steiner, *La Raza: The Mexican Americans*. New York: Harper & Row, 1969.
10. Quoted in Peter Matthiessen, *Sal Si Puedes: Cesar Chavez and the New American Revolution*. New York: Random House, 1969.
11. Quoted in Matthiessen, *Sal Si Puedes*.
12. Quoted in Matthiessen, *Sal Si Puedes*.
13. Todd Gitlin, *The Sixties: Years of Hope, Days of Rage*. New York: Bantam Books, 1987.
14. Quoted in Betty Schechter, *The Peaceable Revolution*. Boston: Houghton Mifflin, 1963.
15. Earl Shorris, *Latinos: A Biography of the People*. New York: Norton, 1992.
16. Wayne Moquin, quoted in Wayne Moquin and Charles Van Doren, eds., *A Documentary History of the Mexican Americans*. New York: Praeger, 1971.

### Chapter 3: An Impossible Dream

17. Matthiessen, *Sal Si Puedes*.

18. Quoted in Matthiessen, *Sal Si Puedes*.
19. Quoted in Matthiessen, *Sal Si Puedes*.
20. Bardacke, "What Went Wrong with the UFW?"
21. Joan W. Moore and Harry Pachon, *Mexican Americans*. Englewood Cliffs, NJ: Prentice-Hall, 1976.

### Chapter 4: A New Direction

22. Quoted in Steiner, *La Raza*.
23. Quoted in Matthiessen, *Sal Si Puedes*.
24. Quoted in Matthiessen, *Sal Si Puedes*.
25. Quoted in Matthiessen, *Sal Si Puedes*.
26. Quoted in Steiner, *La Raza*.
27. Quoted in Steiner, *La Raza*.
28. Quoted in Levy, *Cesar Chavez*.

### Chapter 5: The War of the Flowers

29. Quoted in Arnold Mayer, "The Grapes of Wrath—Vintage 1961," *The Reporter*, February 2, 1961.
30. Quoted in Steiner, *La Raza*.
31. Quoted in Matthiessen, *Sal Si Puedes*.
32. Quoted in Matthiessen, *Sal Si Puedes*.
33. Quoted in Levy, *Cesar Chavez*.
34. Quoted in Steiner, *La Raza*.

### Chapter 6: No Turning Back

35. Quoted in Levy, *Cesar Chavez*.
36. Quoted in Levy, *Cesar Chavez*.
37. Quoted in Steiner, *La Raza*.
38. Matthiessen, *Sal Si Puedes*.
39. Quoted in Levy, *Cesar Chavez*.
40. Jack London, "Definition of a Scab," quoted in Levy, *Cesar Chavez*.
41. Quoted in Levy, *Cesar Chavez*.
42. Quoted in Levy, *Cesar Chavez*.
43. Quoted in Levy, *Cesar Chavez*.

### Chapter 7: Baptisms of Fire

44. Quoted in Matthiessen, *Sal Si Puedes*.
45. Quoted in Levy, *Cesar Chavez*.

46. Quoted in Matthiessen, *Sal Si Puedes.*
47. Quoted in Levy, *Cesar Chavez.*
48. Quoted in Levy, *Cesar Chavez.*

### Chapter 8: Matters of Survival

49. Quoted in Levy, *Cesar Chavez.*
50. Quoted in Levy, *Cesar Chavez.*
51. Quoted in Matthiessen, *Sal Si Puedes.*
52. Quoted in Matthiessen, *Sal Si Puedes.*
53. Quoted in Steiner, *La Raza.*
54. Quoted in Levy, *Cesar Chavez.*

### Chapter 9: Times of Sacrifice and Sorrow

55. Quoted in Levy, *Cesar Chavez.*
56. Steiner, *La Raza.*
57. Quoted in Levy, *Cesar Chavez.*
58. Quoted in Levy, *Cesar Chavez.*
59. Quoted in Levy, *Cesar Chavez.*

60. Quoted in Levy, *Cesar Chavez.*
61. Quoted in Steiner, *La Raza.*

### Chapter 10: A Living Legend

62. Steiner, *La Raza.*
63. Quoted in Matthiessen, *Sal Si Puedes.*
64. Bardacke, "What Went Wrong with the UFW?"
65. Quoted in Marcos Breton, "Fields of Betrayal? Chavez, UFW Neglect Farm Workers, Critics Say," *Sacramento Bee*, February 23, 1992.
66. *Sacramento Bee*, April 24, 1993.
67. Dan Walters, "Cesar Chavez, Mystery Man," *Sacramento Bee*, April 24, 1993.
68. Quoted in Rick Rodriguez, "Farm Workers, Celebrities to Pay Last Respects," *Sacramento Bee*, April 29, 1993.
69. Quoted in Rick Rodriguez, "Thirty-Five Thousand Bid Farewell to Farm Labor Leader," *Sacramento Bee*, April 30, 1993.

# For Further Reading

Jerry Bornstein, *Unions in Transition.* Englewood Cliffs, NJ: Julian Messner, 1981. The history and current prospects of the trade union movement in America.

George D. Horwitz and Paul Fusco, *La Causa: The California Grape Strike.* New York: Collier Books, 1970. Photo-illustrated interviews with participants in the Great Grape Strike—what it felt like to "be there" and help to make that history.

Jacques Levy, *Cesar Chavez: Autobiography of La Causa.* New York: Norton, 1975. The official Chavez biography, by a journalist who became part of the movement to do his research from the inside out.

Peter Matthiessen, *Sal Si Puedes: Cesar Chavez and the New American Revolution.* New York: Random House, 1969. A beautifully written look at Chavez, the man, and the early days of the movement he founded.

Betty Schechter, *The Peaceable Revolution.* Boston: Houghton Mifflin, 1963. A study of the principles of nonviolence, through biographies of men like Henry David Thoreau, M. K. Gandhi, and Martin Luther King Jr.

Earl Shorris, *Latinos: A Biography of the People.* New York: Norton, 1992. A big, readable book about the Latino experience. Older students will find it as entertaining as any novel.

Thomas Sowell, *Ethnic America: A History.* New York: Basic Books, 1981. Looks at ethnic diversity as it has shaped the American experience.

# Additional Works Consulted

Fred Alvarez, "A Growing Influence," *Los Angeles Times*, October 17, 1993. Commentary on the renewed importance of labor contractors in California agriculture.

B. L. Baer, "Good, Brave, and Stubborn Man," *Nation*, October 25, 1975. Excellent profile of Chavez as activist, organizer, and human being.

G. Baker, "Teamster Raid: Stalled in the Vineyards," *Ramparts*, December 1974. Critical view of Teamster tactics in the jurisdictional disputes with UFW.

Frank Bardacke, "What Went Wrong with the UFW?" *Sacramento Bee*, August 1, 1993. Well-written examination of UFW problems in the changing labor market of the eighties.

Marcos Breton, "Fields of Betrayal? Chavez, UFW Neglect Farm Workers, Critics Say," *Sacramento Bee*, February 23, 1992. Overview of criticisms levied at Chavez and the organizational structure of the union.

J. G. Dunne, "To Die Standing. Cesar Chavez and the Chicanos," *Atlantic Monthly*, June 1971. A Study of Chavez and his place in Mexican-American culture during the late sixties.

Ernesto Galarza, *Merchants of Labor: The Mexican Bracero Story*. Santa Barbara, CA: McNally and Loftin, 1964. Thorough and scholarly history of all stages of the bracero programs and their impact on southwestern agriculture.

————, "Program for Action," *Common Ground*, Summer 1949.

M. K. Gandhi, *Non-Violent Resistance*. Ahmedabad, India: Navajwan Trust, 1951. English edition: Schocken Books, New York, 1967.

Todd Gitlin, *The Sixties: Years of Hope, Days of Rage*. New York: Bantam Books, 1987. A history of the social and political struggles of the sixties, written by an activist who was a leader of Students for a Democratic Society (SDS).

Juan Gonzales, *Mexican-American Farm Workers: The California Agricultural Industry*. Westport, CT: Praeger, 1985. A look at the contribution of Mexican and Mexican-American campesinos from a scholarly, sociological perspective.

Martin Luther King Jr., *Stride Toward Freedom: The Montgomery Story*. New York: Harper & Row, 1958. Dr. King's own account of the Montgomery bus boycott.

S. Kushner, "Cesar Chavez: Far from Defeated," *Christian Century*, November 13, 1974. Looks at Chavez's courageous response to the reversals and misfortunes of UFW.

Joan W. Moore and Harry Pachon, *Mexican Americans*. Englewood Cliffs, NJ: Prentice-Hall, 1976. Sociological study of Mexican Americans as an identifiable ethnic group in the "mainstream" of U.S. culture.

Wayne Moquin and Charles Van Doren, eds., *A Documentary History of the Mexican Americans*. New York: Praeger, 1971.

*Newsweek*, "Boost for Chavez," May 26, 1975. One of a number of national articles about the struggles of Cesar Chavez and UFW in the seventies.

Rick Rodriguez, "35,000 Bid Farewell to Farm Labor Leader," *Sacramento Bee*, April 30, 1993. Newsfeature on memorial services at the United Farm Workers compound in Delano.

Sam Stanton, "Farm Workers' Leader Cesar Chavez, 66, Dies," *Sacramento Bee*, April 24, 1993. News story on the death of Chavez, with comments from friends, coworkers, and even opponents who knew and admired him.

Kevin Starr, *Americans and the California Dream, 1850–1915*. New York: Oxford University Press, 1973. An often entertaining history of California, with emphasis on the colorful characters who helped to shape its identity.

Stan Steiner, *La Raza: The Mexican Americans*. New York: Harper & Row, 1969. A distinctly personal look at La Raza and its influence on Mexican-American life in the strident sixties.

*Time*, "Inspiration, Sí; Administration, No," April 22, 1974. Early article questioning the structure of UFW as a functioning labor union rather than an inspirational movement.

United Farm Workers of America, *The Indestructible Spirit of the United Farm Workers of America AFL-CIO*. Keene, CA: UFW, undated.

*U.S. News & World Report*, "Chavez vs. the Teamsters: Farm Workers' Historic Vote," September 22, 1975. National perspective on the election struggles between UFW and Teamsters.

Luis Valdez, "Tribute: Dolores Huerta," *Image*, August 12, 1990.

Dan Walters, "Cesar Chavez: Mystery Man," *Sacramento Bee*, April 24, 1993. A regular columnist for the *Bee* reflects on the meaning of Chavez's life and death.

John O. West, *Mexican-American Folklore*. Little Rock, AR: August House, 1988. Collection of songs, jokes, stories, customs, and superstitions of Mexican-American communities in the southwestern United States.

# Index

# Picture Credits

Cover photo: AP/Wide World Photos

© Alan Pogue, 11, 95

AP/Wide World, 24, 30, 39, 41, 59, 99

Archives of Labor and Urban Affairs, Wayne State University, 13, 16, 18, 21, 23, 27, 32, 35, 43, 44, 48, 50, 52, 55, 57, 58, 60, 61 (both), 63, 66, 68, 69, 70, 71, 72, 73, 75, 78, 80, 83, 85, 88, 90, 92, 94, 97

U.S. Department of Agriculture, 28

# About the Author

Linda Jacobs Altman specializes in writing history and biography for young people. Her recent books include *The Pullman Strike of 1894: Turning Point for American Labor*, *Migrant Workers: The Temporary People*, and *Mr. Darwin's Voyage*. She lives in the small town of Clearlake, California, with her husband Richard.